THE NEW WORLD GOVERNMENT

STRUCTURE
AND
CONSTITUTION

Authored by
Prof. Dr. D. Swaminadhan
Global Chair
World Intellectual Forum (WIF)
Hyderabad, India
E-mail: worldintellectualforum@gmail.com

THE NEW WORLD GOVERNMENT-STRUCTURE AND CONSTITUTION

PROF. DR. D. SWAMINADHAN

LIBRARY OF CONGRESS CONTROL NUMBER: 2019902698
ISBN: HARDCOVER   978-1-7960-0142-6
             SOFTCOVER   978-1-7960-0141-9
             EBOOK   978-1-7960-0140-2

Print information available on the last page.

Rev. date: 03/23/2019

To order additional copies of this book, contact:
Xlibris
1-800-455-039
www.Xlibris.com.au
Orders@Xlibris.com.au
787076

CONTENTS

DEDICATION

The author wishes to dedicate his book to all those war heroes of the First and Second World Wars who sacrificed their lives for the sake of their countries.

- The Author

FOREWORD

The situation of contemporary world peace and security is quite alarming. Nuclear holocaust and a third world war seem to be imminent given the present world situation. The total number of ready-to-use nuclear warheads currently is huge, but only a few of them would be enough for humanity forever to cease to exist. Such countries as USA, Russia, France, China, UK, India, Pakistan, Israel, and North Korea have the ability, with the help of detonation of such bombs, to destroy the whole of humanity unless bound by constraint, compassion, and human values and concerns. Now the worst seems to have come to take place. The situation in Syria is getting out of control, and the conflict between UK and Russia is now becoming extended to include USA, Russia, UK, Iran, Israel, and Syria. The situation in the Korean peninsula is also alarming, although for the time being, it has abated. The trade war between USA and China; the triple standoff between USA, Israel, and Iran; and the conflict in Yemen and other places seem to be going out of control. The USA flexes its muscles and threatens trade wars with Europe unless we disengage from trading with Iran. All will be engulfed in a nuclear holocaust if world war three breaks out. It is also alarming that the Committee of Atomic Scientists, which includes fifteen Nobel Prize winners, on January 25, this year, decided to reduce in 2018 the symbolic time before the end of the world for another half a minute. Now only two symbolic minutes are left until the world's Armageddon. The doomsday clock is an internationally recognized symbolic indicator of how close we are to the destroying our earth civilization through dangerous technologies of our own production. They are nuclear, chemical, and biological weapons, but besides this, there are new global threats including the effect on climate change by modern industrial societies causing global warming and weather chaos. There are also problems caused by new biotechnologies and cyber-technologies, which can be misused and applied towards military and violent purposes and then cause irreparable damage, whether by intention, miscalculation, or accident, to our way of life and the planet as a whole. Scientific technology itself has become like 'The Sorcerer's Apprentice'

('Der Zauberlehrling'), described first in the fairy poem by Goethe, who could not control the demons that originally he invoked to serve him. Interestingly, Marx and Engels also invoked Goethe's poem in their *The Communist Manifesto* by saying that modern capitalist society is like 'the sorcerer who is no longer able to control the powers of the nether world whom he has called up by his spells.' We all know this. The situation is way out of hand. But what can we do about it? Marxism was tried, but it didn't really work. So what do we do next? One thing by the way we can do is recover the lost transcendental socialism that was the original vision of Marxism before harsh materialism overtook it, when Moses Hess introduced Marx and Engels to each other, and he and Marx both worked on the *Rheinische Zeitung* as editors. Moses Hess began his intellectual career as a left Hegelian, along with Ruge, Marx, Engels, Cieszkowski, David Strauss, Rudolf Haym, and others, who based his ideas on his Jewish faith and the pantheism of Spinoza, Hegel, and Fichte, as he saw it, and believed that there would eventually come about on earth a society lacking distinctions of class and wealth in which there would be no contradictions between private passion and public law: external compulsion would not be needed as mankind gradually became collectively and individually enlightened. He worked for what he saw as the social expression of pantheism and the dialectical development of the self-realisation of the Absolute Spirit in history. He put these ideas into his early work *Die Heilege Gesichte der Menschheit* (Stuttgart 1837). This work, *The Sacred History of Mankind,* argued that there had now to be a new covenant for mankind and that history was moving towards a time when there was to be a final reconciliation of the human race, a free and equal society based on mutual love and the community of goods. His vision of communism was essentially spiritual first and foremost. His next important work, *The European Triarchy* (1841), based his vision of a communist society on his reading of Hegelian philosophy (Hegel had meanwhile died in 1831). Like later Marx, Hess wanted to combine German speculative thought and French political intelligence into a common formula for all of Europe. For this to happen, the philosophy of action had to replace mere theorising. Hess met Marx in the autumn of 1841, and they worked together for some years as friends and collaborators, but then Marx, as so often happened, quarrelled with Hess. Towards the end of his life, Moses Hess moved to Paris and wrote there other important works and played an interesting role in French intellectual life. If only Hess's vision of transcendental socialism had won out over Marx's grim economic deterministic vision, we might not now be in the mess we find ourselves as a planet!

But we are where we are, and all global inhabitants and their governments and the global governance systems should urgently apply their minds on how to not only prevent the third world war situation but also initiate short- and long-term measures to forestall such catastrophic situations including those arising out of climate change, misapplied cyber-technologies, and misusing modern technology and scientific knowledge for militarism and war. We have to wake up as a planet and realise that war and violence are no longer a feasible or acceptable way of solving political disputes and differences. Yet the mindsets of our respective nationalist leaders and governments seem still wedded to the idea of 'victoryism'—if only we build more weapons or spy on more people using ever more sophisticated espionage systems, victory will be 'ours.' But perhaps we should realise with Mahavira and Gandhi and Christ that, in fact, true victory is the victory we can achieve over our own lower selves, over our own ignorance. True victory is enlightenment. This is what the Druids of old used to teach to the Celtic tribes, some of the fiercest warriors known to history, and it is what the Rishis of ancient India taught to the Kshatriyas.

Somehow, therefore, we have to think through the structures that a future world system might have to enable victory for all of us and that enables more and more people to achieve self-mastery and enlightenment. Somehow, we need to find geopolitical structures and agreements that put in place mechanisms that enable mankind to finally realise our long-held dreams of world peace, fraternity, and equality. The current world system is holding and has so far prevented world war three through the work of the United Nations and its various subsidiary organisations. But there is a sense amongst us that there is a need for the replacement or augmentation of the United Nations as it appears to be failing to solve all of today's complex global problems. One particular problem is that the UN was designed for a world of interlocking nation states and can help solve (most) wars between nations, but since most of today's wars are now civil wars, it has no real mechanism for resolving them. Either we can build new structures into the UN system or we can think outside the box and develop an entirely new world governmental system as an alternative to UNO. Or we can do both at the same time.

In this book, the author has done the latter operation and has presented a new approach for the formation of a New Federal Democratic World Government. The author has presented this proposal in his capacity as global chair of the World Intellectual Forum, which he has inaugurated in India with his colleague, swami professor S. A. R. P. V. Chaturvedi, global co-chair, to think through some of the most complex challenges facing the global community at the present time. A scientist and civil servant of many years standing, Dr. Swaminadhan is to be commended for his imaginative and yet realistic approach as evidenced in this book. In fact, in the World Intellectual Forum, we have currently at least three members with proposals for world government, which also include proposals put forward by Prof. Glen T. Martin and also Igor Kondrashin. I will try briefly and summarise what is different about Dr. Swaminadhan's approach.

For Swaminadhan, the formation of the New Federal World Parliament is to be through proportional representation of each nation's parliaments, and thus this avoids direct election processes for its formation. He suggested two methods for calculating the proportionality. The first method is to calculate the proportionality on the basis of the countries' share of world population as indicated in annexure 2. This method shows wide variations in the countries' contribution of MPs because of their huge population differences. This, however, gives the controlling majority to China and India, the world's two most populist nations, and means that if ever China and India made a diplomatic treaty, or the one conquered the other, they could hold the entire world to ransom and establish a global dictatorship. I foresee a problem with this, therefore, and doubt that other smaller nations would be happy to accept it. This is the advantage of the current United Nations system, which is that each nation, great or small, has its own recognised sovereignty guaranteed, at least in theory. The second method is to calculate the proportionality on the basis of the six continents and their countries (annexure 4). This method of continental proportion of MPs makes all countries equal in contributing of MPs to the World Parliament. The problem, of course, is how and when the UN recognises emergent nations (such as Scotland, Catalonia, or Palestine) and what it does when existing nations bully or oppress newly emerging nations. Dr. Swaminadhan's book, even though, does not address this problem specifically, such any other problems could probably be solved using the authority of the world government. But simply Dr. Swaminadhan's perhaps assumes that once it is in place, the world will simply accept, in a transitionless phase, the shift to his proposed system of world government. It is hard for me to see how this phase will be so easy. Even in the UK, where we have been members of a regional organisation, the European Union, for many years, easily stirred up propaganda and has led to a resurgence of fake nationalist ideologies that is in danger of pushing us out of a union that has guaranteed peace and stability in Europe as a whole for years. So it will be hard to see why the existing nations of the world will accept world government so easily or bloodlessly. Political scientists would say that power, which is the currency of politics, does not shift its 'work' parameters so swiftly. And when people have power, they are reluctant to either share it or hand it over. But I admire Dr. Swaminadhan's eternal optimism and his belief that people will be rational enough to see that world federal government is the only lasting solution to the world's many problems. I remember first hearing about the idea of world federal government in Canada in about 1979 and becoming a convert to the cause. But that was forty years ago, and we seem to be no nearer now than we did then. Around that time, I wrote a paper about the etymology of the word 'federalism' and discovered that it came from the basic root word 'fides,' meaning 'faith.' Without some kind of common faith, a federal system, in fact, will be impossible. But what exactly is this common faith that humanity is striving after?

In Dr. Swaminadhan's book, the World Parliament will have only two houses—the upper house (Elders' House) and the lower house. This is modelled on the UK House of Lords and House of Commons, or the India Rajya Sabha and Lok Sabha. This is a good idea in principle, but it is not explained exactly how power is to be shared between them. Perhaps a standing committee of both the houses of parliament may look in to this issue, or perhaps we need a World Constitutional Convention to bring together all the proponents of the various world federal government schemes currently on the table and then decide which is the best to adopt or whether it is possible to synthesise the best of them. This could perhaps be a job for the World Intellectual Forum? It could even take place in India, the world's largest true democracy.

The list of continents he gives is as follows:

No	Name	Number of countries
1.	Asia	50
2.	Africa	54
3.	North America	23
4.	South America	12
5.	Europe	51
6.	Australia	14

I find some geographical difficulties with the above list of continents, speaking personally, and suggest instead an alternative list:

1. Africa
2. Europe
3. Asia
4. The Americas (counted as one continent—North, Central, and South Americas)
5. Oceania, Australasia, and Antarctica
6. Eurasia (Russia, Commonwealth of Independent States)

There is also a problem with the above continents schema, which is how to give Russia adequate representation. I suggest therefore that perhaps Russia and the Commonwealth of Independent States be considered a continent all on its own, called Eurasia, and not split in two, so we would then have six continents in total. But these are technical matters that political geographers can pore over to agree the details later on.

It would be a helpful addition to a future edition of this book if we could have maps showing us the various areas and regions in full, since geographers will need to get to work on drawing the boundary lines. After all, when British map maker George Everest went into the Himalayas to map the boundary of Nepal and China, he also discovered Mount Everest to be the highest mountain in the world, and so maps are an important aspect of today's geopolitical realities, so if we are serious about finding a formula for world federal government that everybody will accept, we better get the geographical details right and agree on the maps.

SWAMINADHAN EXPLAINS

The upper house is presided over by the chairman assisted by five deputy chairmen representing the five continental areas and to be elected by the house.

The lower house is presided over by the speaker assisted by five deputy speakers representing the other five continental areas. They will be elected by the lower house.

With a view to have wider dispersal of world capital cities, six world capital cities—one primary and five secondary world capital cities—will be established in six continental areas.

Either it is presumed that the World Parliament will decide the above areas, regions and locations of capital cities, in consultation with the work of professional political geographers and cartographers, or a World Constitutional Convention could discuss, debate, and decide this complex issue. Boundary disputes are, in fact, a huge cause of wars and conflict, and so in the matter of Kashmir, for example, or Tibet/India or Sahel/Morocco or even Slovenia/Croatia or Palestine/Israel or Scotland/England over north seas oil resources, etc., there are huge ongoing boundary disputes. It is unlikely even a world government will be able to resolve these differences amicably overnight. Is it right for intellectuals to suggest these answers are going to be easy to solve when, for centuries, learned people, geographers, and political thinkers have failed to resolve them? Perhaps our job as intellectuals is to point out that ego attachment to boundaries is ultimately futile, an exercise that is false reification? Where exactly is the border between Europe and Asia? Between Africa and Asia? Between the Pacific and Atlantic oceans? Should we fight about it? Or should we not rather meditate together on the vagaries and impermanence of the shifting sands of time. And should we not realise with a jolt: the earth is already one; it is just that we haven't caught up yet.

Also, when Swaminadhan says that 'all the nations and their people's representatives are involved in the formation of the World Parliament and the World Government which is a welcome feature,' he leaves out the fact there are also regional assemblies of governments, such as the European Union, already in place on planet Earth and there is also the African Union, which already groups all fifty-five African nations into a regional organisation working for peace, prosperity, and justice for all Africans. There is also the Organization of American States (comprising all thirty-five American countries) and other similar organisations all over the world, including one that is trying to get going in Asia (Asia Cooperation Dialogue, ACD). Perhaps organisations like this can play a role in helping mankind transition from an era of competing states to an era of cooperating world governance?

Most importantly, Dr Swaminadhan's outline of the proposed World Constitution includes adherence to the fourfold principles:

a)	justice	-	socioeconomic and political
b)	liberty	-	of thought, expression, belief, and faith
c)	equality	-	of opportunity and status
d)	fraternity	-	promote amongst all nations unity and integrity, assuring freedom and dignity of people and nations

These are certainly admirable goals and ideals that should govern any world governmental proposal likely to be acceptable to the broad masses of humanity.

I would probably add several other principles myself, including:

e)	dignity	-	the right to be treated at all times with dignity and respect no matter one's station in life
f)	responsibility	-	of action and thought that each of us has duties and responsibilities to one another, of care, compassion, and mutual aid, including the duty of becoming educated in the civic, intellectual, moral, and spiritual virtues

A further important element in Dr. Swaminadhan's constitution is that it includes the following:

DIRECTIVE PRINCIPLES FOR THE NEW WORLD GOVERNMENT

It shall be the aim of the world government to secure certain other rights for all inhabitants within the world government but without immediate guarantee of universal achievement and enforcement. These rights are defined as directive principles, obligating the world government to pursue every reasonable mean for universal realization and implementation and shall include the following:

1. equal opportunity for useful employment for everyone, with wages or remuneration sufficient to assure human dignity

2. freedom of choice in work, occupation, employment, or profession
3. full access to information and to the accumulated knowledge of the human race;
4. free and adequate public education available to everyone, extending to the pre-university level; equal opportunities for elementary and higher education for all persons; equal opportunity for continued education for all persons throughout life; the right of any person or parent to choose a private educational institution at any time
5. free and adequate public health services and medical care available to everyone throughout life under conditions of free choice
6. equal opportunity for leisure time for everyone; better distribution of the work load of society so that every person may have equitable leisure time opportunities
7. equal opportunity for everyone to enjoy the benefits of scientific and technological discoveries and developments
8. protection for everyone against the hazards and perils of technological innovations and developments
9. protection of the natural environment, which is the common heritage of humanity against pollution, ecological disruption, or damage, which could imperil life or lower the quality of life
10. conservation of those natural resources of earth that are limited so that present and future generations may continue to enjoy life on the planet Earth.

These are incredibly important principles and directives that should govern the workings of the world government, according to Dr. Swaminadhan's constitution. As an educator and founder of Education Aid, who used to work at the Institute of Education in London University, I agree wholeheartedly with the directives enunciated above. UNESCO should also wholeheartedly endorse them. Once we put education and scientific research above our addiction to power and ignorance and fear and violence, then we will have proved worthy of achieving a state of world governance.

Another interesting feature of Dr. Swaminadhan's world government system is that it will include

a) the World Army,
b) the World Intelligence Agency, and
c) the World Police System.

These are interesting ideas, and of the army proposal, Swaminadhan says, 'The World Government will have a World Army to intervene in wars or conflicts between countries and to take care of defence in case of inter-planetary conflicts.' This is the first time I have seen in print any world government proposal including the possibility of interplanetary conflicts, but if you think about it, it is fairly logical. If there is intelligent life teeming throughout the universe, there is no guarantee it would all be friendly to humanity. After all, we are not always even friendly to ourselves!

On the national army of each country, Swaminadhan says, 'Each Nation will prune its existing National Army strength and contribute to the World Army. They may continue to maintain their Security and Intelligence Structures.' This is a brilliant idea and one that gets my full support. Most countries around the world are attached to their armies—with all their uniforms, their flags, and their battle honours. The British army, for example, is proud of all its different regimental histories and their battle honours, and so too is the India army, which was trained initially into being by British army officers, as was that of Pakistan. So in Swaminadhan's brilliant idea, these armies can continue, but on voluntary level, governments may give a proportion of their military expenditure towards the bringing into being of a World Army. One imagines there would be intense discussion about how this can be done persuasively. My own Leonardo da Vinci Peace Prize, to develop the Nonagon project, to cap the Pentagon with a new nine-sided department of peace, is one way, by shifting military budget spending worldwide to include at a stroke 50 per cent for peacemaking and war-ending purposes. Some of this shifted money could perhaps also go towards the funding of a genuine World Army.

Of the World Police System, Swaminadhan says that to maintain law and order, the world government will have a World Police System. That is all well and good, but there is a worrying trend in societies around the world to see police given more and more powers and the ability to enter people's houses, arrest them, and do all manner of harassment without their being answerable to anybody. I would only agree to some kind of World Police System coming into place as long as ordinary people in a kind of jury system had a strong control over what it was doing and that individual officers could be called to account easily if they overstepped their duties. Too often around the world, police forces are corrupt and extract all kinds of protection money from people. The World Police System must be free of all this and must be transparent in its workings. It would also have to have the power to investigate and overrule the work of local police forces, so where individual policemen are indeed being corrupt or colluding with injustice and criminality, ordinary people could bring into the world police and they could then investigate not only the crime itself but also the local police who have so far failed to solve it.

Dr. Swaminadhan also says the world government will maintain a World Intelligence Agency for intelligence and security. This again is an important idea, but my only stipulation here would be that this World Intelligence Agency would be sworn to nonviolence and would restrict itself purely to information finding and intelligence gathering, against criminals and evil people and organisations worldwide. It would have very high standards of ethics, and it would not be allowed to engage in secret assassinations or covert killings like the CIA and other existing intelligence organisations do regularly. On the contrary, to every state that acceded to the world government system, it would have the right to investigate their own national intelligence agents and to pursue agents who themselves might have broken cosmic or moral laws. But this World Intelligence Agency would have to recruit people of only truly globalist values who put love of peace and justice above all possible corruptions or nationalist tendencies. Where are such people to be found when our educational systems are in the hands of national governments and their bureaucracies?

On another matter, Dr. Swaminadhan's constitution has several organisations continuing to exist even after the world government is formally declared, such as the World Bank (WB), International Monetary Fund (IMF), World Health Organisation (WHO), World Food Organisation (WFO), and other similar world bodies that will continue to exist under the proposed world government.

In fact, here, again, I cannot really agree with Dr. Swaminadhan and suggest he rethinks this part. The World Bank and the International Monetary Fund have wreaked untold damage on natural ecosystems and national economies worldwide and have been part of an enforced privatisation scheme, for example, which have made life difficult for many countries around the world. I would much rather see these two organisations abolished and a fresh start brought in for international economic relations. As long as the World Bank and the IMF run things, life will be good for the rich and powerful at the top of the pyramid of power and continue to be grim and tragic for the billions toiling away at the bottom of the pyramid of power. What we really need on this planet is what I call 'transcendental socialism,' which is a form of socialism rooted in the cosmic laws of compassion, love, cooperation, and sharing in which the genius of each citizen on earth can be fulfilled and nurtured for the common good.

Rather than shutting down all UN agencies, however, I would much rather, for example, that UNESCO not only carry on into the new era of the one world federal government system but also have a new structure whereby projects and initiatives can also be taken directly by world citizens worldwide, through a federal assembly, as well as by individual government's ambassadors. This would further democratise UNESCO, which sometimes is perhaps too state centred in its work.

As global chairman of the World Intellectual Forum, Dr. Swaminadhan is to be commended for this timely study, and his contribution should be read with care by all those who wish to see an ordered transition to a more sensible and intelligent world order than is currently the case.

At the founding meeting of the World Intellectual Forum, I asked a question about world government proposals—namely, how can different world government proposals cooperate?

I went on to explain that this seems important especially to the work of the World Intellectual Forum, since we have several possibilities being mooted amongst our members. There are many proposals around, including (1) the World Constitution and Parliament Association of Prof. Glen Martin, founded by Philip Isely (whom I once met); (2) the proposal of Dr. Igor Kondrashin called the Universal State of the Earth, Supreme Council of Humanity; (3) Nicholas Haggar's proposal for the United Federation of the World (he is also chair of the Supreme Council of Humanity); (4) the World Federalists Association, 'Montreux Declaration; The Principles for World Federal Government,' World Federalist Movement–Institute for Global Policy; (5) Regional Federalists (Gradualists) (e.g., the Federalists [Italy, http://www.thefederalist.eu], Federal Trust for Education and Research [UK], Union of European Federalists, Pulse for Europe, Movimento Federalista Europeo, European Movement, European Union, etc.); (6) Association of World Citizens (Rene Wadlow, president); (7) Campaign for a More Democratic United Nations (CAMDUN) (i.e., reform the UN first and make it more accountable and democratic); (8) the Great Transition Initiative (Prof. Luis Cabrera); (9) newly emerging nations (e.g., Kurdistan, Catalan, Palestine, Scotland) and Leopold Kohr's *Breakdown of Nations;* (10) World Spiritual Assembly (Lama Gangchen) / Congress of Leaders of World and Traditional Religions (President Narabayev), World Parliament of Religions; (11) the International Monarchist League / Council of Monarchs; (12) ecological models towards global environmental and human co-governance (World Environment Organization proposal, Green Cross); and (13) Dr. Swaminadhan also has presented us with a model of his own for future world government to consider and has written this model up in more detail in the current book.

Is it possible for all these models and paradigms towards 'world government' or 'world governance' to coexist, not just in the WIF but in the wider world? Are they compatible or oppositional or incompatible? Some are gradualist and regional (e.g., focusing on European Union); some are globalist, some advocate a world republic, some advocate keeping constitutional monarchies, etc. Then there is the whole question, should we be talking about world government or world governance? In my paper to the World Intellectual Forum in Hyderabad in December 2017, I asked if promoting world government is actually the business of philosophers.

I went on to say that I don't think it is the main business of philosophers. Cicero mentions it. Posidonius mentions it. Alexander the Great mentions it as an idea he was promoting through his military conquest of all nations. Caesar mentioned it as an idea he was bringing in through his conquests and his kingly ambitions. Roman Republicans like Cicero, Pompey, and Varro believed a rational world order would eventually emerge—a Pax Romana Republica. But I personally rule out violent conquest attempts as valid. The ancient Pharaohs believed in it as synonymous with Egyptian expansionism. The Zoroastrian Persian rulers mentioned it as they sought to conquer the Greeks and extend their frontiers in every direction. The Hebrew prophets dreamed of it but as a spiritual fact in which their deity would rule amongst all other deities and their priesthoods would be reckoned the most powerful on earth, and so on. Christians mentioned it in promoting their idea that Jesus was actually the Lord of the Heavenly Kingdom to come to earth, to usher in an eventual era of world spiritual governance and peace once everyone on earth accepts his lordship—he had earned this title, say Christians, by his teachings, his cruel death, and his supernatural resurrection from death, and now rules from a heavenly kingdom, which you need clairvoyant eyes of faith to perceive (like Osiris to the Egyptians). Buddhists argued something very similar—Buddha is the world ruler of our epoch, the dharma rajah, and all good people seeking enlightenment will support and assist his spreading of the dharma to prevent global catastrophe. Hindu sages believe that Satya yuga will return to earth and only then will we have a world governance, because then we will all individually be following the rules of virtue—prompted from within, by our own consciences. This was Gandhi and Aurobindo and Ramana Maharshi's idea—the need for outer world government will wither away as we all become more prone to enlightenment. Dr. Raghavan N. Iyer also said something similar in his work *Parapolitics.* The theosophical tradition also argues something similar. So have thinkers such as William Irwin Thomson. British philosophers long believed that they could turn eventually the British Empire, or British Commonwealth, into the seeds of a world governance system based on rational federal principles (Lionel Curtis, Cecil Rhodes, William Beveridge, etc.). Modern-day Indian leaders also believed in world federal government as a realistic goal (Pandit Nehru). It seems to me that philosophers have been advocating different forms of world government for a very long time—but this is only one branch of philosophy; let us call it global political philosophy. There are also epistemology, ethics, philosophy of religion, metaphysics, eschatology, comparative theology, philosophy of mind, philosophy of love, philosophy of education, and philosophy of art and literature; all these are also important fields of philosophical activity. All of them are also involved, directly or indirectly, in the search for peace. The search for peace is not the sole prerogative of political philosophy. That itself is a cultural bias of modernity.

So perhaps encouraging, fostering, and educating for self-governance is the real business of philosophers? What about world self-government? What about world autarchy? What would that be like? This I argue is what the true sages of mankind seemed to have argued for. Plato, Pythagoras, Socrates, Gandhi, Jesus, Christ, Buddha, Mahavira, Sankara, Ramanuja, Kant, Hegel, Tolstoy, Thoreau, Romain Rolland, Lanzo del Vasta, and many others have argued that the root of peace, the bedrock, will be achieved when mankind as a whole becomes virtuous. Philosophy is conceived in this tradition as a school of virtue formation. Once people know the importance of truth and integrity in them and realise the eschatological context in which our ethical choices are framed, then we naturally gravitate towards ethical decisions in our lives. If we have power, then we must come to exercise our powers ethically and not egotistically, but only if we have achieved enlightened self-government—that is, have conquered our negative characteristics and qualities and triumphed over the inner ignorance we all carry around inside us.

However, I think both approaches are compatible. Just as in the work of the World Intellectual Forum, we have several approaches to world government, so too we have several approaches to virtue formation and global education. One thing is certain, which is that until we get more international awareness and globalist consciousness arising in peoples, less fear and tribalism, we are not going to get peace on planet Earth. So the work of Professor Chumakov in advocating global studies is a key part of our raising awareness worldwide about the need for comparative thinking through our common problems.

Dr. Igor Kondrashin has a different concept in his work and seems to want to leapfrog to a global aristocratic body that will assume the governance of the world at an elite level and include religious saviours and messiahs giving spiritual direction to humanity. This is a very platonic solution to the problems of world chaos, but how realistic is it that it will ever be accepted? I think Dr. Swaminadhan strays more to the democratic understanding of politics, and Dr. Kondrashin strays more to an aristocratic understanding of politics in a way more reminiscent of Nietzsche. This is the beauty of the World Intellectual Forum—it is a very broad church.

What is not altogether clear to the unbiased reader is what Dr. Swaminadhan feels the need to propose a rival project to that pursued by Dr. Glen Martin as president of the World Constitution and Parliament Association. The World Parliament project is a democratic, nonmilitary, federal world government based on establishing peace and solving environmental problems. The World Parliament project has three houses (Peoples, Counsellors, Nations), plus the world executive, the world judiciary, the world administration, and spiritual liaisons. In the World Parliament proposal of Dr. Glen Martin, the World Parliament is in three parts: one, the House of Peoples, elected directly by the people equally from one thousand world electoral and administrative districts. Then there is a House of Nations, appointed or elected by national governments. Finally, there is a House of Counsellors of two hundred elected by the other two houses, chosen for their global perspective; which has nominative, consultative, initiative, and referral functions. This is confusing because in one diagram, this House of Counsellors is elected by universities and colleges around the world. Some aspects of the WCPA system are different to that of Dr. Swaminadhan, whose system will retain a World Army and Intelligence System. But for the WCPA, there is to be no World Army or Intelligence Service; instead, there will be an emphasis on *disarmament*, which nations are expected to accomplish when the earth constitution is ratified. The world government will not retain or use weapons of mass destruction. Although this seems admirable and decidedly utopian, in fact, Dr. Swaminadhan's proposal here has probably more chance of being accepted in the short to medium term. Indeed, Dr. Glen T Martin's constitution asks the nations of the world to simply dissolve all their intelligence services at a stroke but doesn't explain what will be replacing them.

Article 4 of the WCPA Earth Constitution includes the following:

1. prevent wars and armed conflicts amongst the nations, regions, districts, parts, and peoples of earth
2. supervise disarmament and prevent rearmament; prohibit and eliminate the design, testing, manufacture, sale, purchase, use, and possession of weapons of mass destruction, and prohibit or regulate all lethal weapons that the World Parliament may decide
3. prohibit incitement to war and discrimination against or defamation of conscientious objectors
4. provide the means for peaceful and just solutions of disputes and conflicts amongst or between nations, peoples, and/or other components within the federation of earth
5. supervise boundary settlements and conduct plebiscites as needed

These are totally admirable aims and intentions, and I think most of the citizens of planet Earth would agree to this, but I am not convinced that the nations and people are ready to hand sovereignty over every other aspect of their lives to a world government system.

My own preference would be to develop a gradualist system much as David Mitrany proposed in his functionalist approach to federalism. Let's start putting in place world governance on specific issues and let us, above all, start with peace. Designing and developing a House of Peace whose function would be to do the above five tasks, and which would be ceded power to do this by all the governments of the earth, and the United Nations, and regional bodies such as the EU, would be a huge step in the right direction. If each national government could also develop a department of peace and give it as large a budget as the current departments of defence around the world, that would also be a step in the right direction. Then once each country has a department of peace, they can begin designing and comparing different world governance structures that they prefer and find admirable.

Another approach that I opposed over a decade ago is that a Universal Parliament of Cultures should be represented on a linguistic basis, with each language of the world represented, and which would be made up of intellectuals, writers, poets, philologists, philosophers, and not politicians. The largest linguistic groups should send three delegates, the medium sized send two delegates, and the smallest send one delegate. About four billion of the earth's 6.5 billion people, or over 60 per cent of the earth's population, speak one of the main thirty languages as their native tongue: Chinese (Mandarin), Hindi, Spanish, English, Arabic, Portuguese, Bengali, Russian, Japanese, German, Panjabi, Javanese, Korean, Vietnamese, Telugu, Marathi, Tamil, French, Urdu, Italian, Turkish, Persian, Gujarati, Polish, Ukrainian, Malayalam, Kannada, Oriya, Burmese, and Thai. Add in another of the two hundred most populous languages on the planet and we would have about four hundred delegates to the House of Cultures. Speaking personally as a poet, historian, writer, and philosopher, I prefer this idea of a House of Cultures for organising world unity and amity between peoples. Politicians seem to have too much in their hearts the idea of stirring up enmity and hostility with other cultural groups. Once we have world amity, we will be ready for a world federal government.

I also think there should be a House of Common Values in which the major religious, spiritual, and philosophical traditions of the planet can also assemble and discuss their differences in amicable and meaningful ways and oversee legislation stemming from the World Parliament, although this matter will have to be handled with great sensitivity and care. Perhaps existing interfaith organisations such as the World Congress of Faith and other similar bodies (WCRP, Parliament of Religions, etc.) could play a role here. My own interfaith peace treaty is an attempt to get an initial ceasefire in ongoing religious wars around the planet.

I wonder therefore why these elements are left out of the world government systems of both Dr. Glen Martin and Dr. Swaminadhan? In fact, the World Parliament talks of interfaith advisers/liaisons but never defines their role or gives them any formal status in the Constitution.

So there are elements lacking in both Dr. Martin and Dr. Swaminadhan's constitutional proposals. However, there are many strong points in both of them. There are also some good ideas in Dr. Kondrashin's concepts and other related initiatives.

Fortunately, having now brought the World Intellectual Forum into being, we now have mechanisms for us all to debate the pros and cons of these different proposals and go into fine detail, honing and correcting, improving and sharpening, our various proposals. Gradually, let us hope a world of peace, disarmament, and intellectual cooperation will emerge from the current era of barbarism and darkness.

There are still no mechanisms in place for investigating the causes of major international disasters and incidents such as what happened on 9/11 in the USA. When the Iranian president questioned in the UN General Assembly whether the official Bush narrative that 9/11 was caused simply by Al Qaeda led by Osama Bin Laden is actually true, and when Egyptian president Morsi calls for an international scientific inquiry into establishing the facts behind the 9/11 events, it is a sobering thought that these events then helped lead directly to the invasion of Iraq, the invasion of Afghanistan, the destabilisation of Syria and Libya, and constant sabre rattling by the West against Iran, all without a shred of evidence showing that any of these nations actually had anything to do with 9/11 whatsoever. It is as if the world has been led into a weird *Alice in Wonderland* world where everything is in reverse and 9/11 was the day we all fell down the rabbit hole. In the Jaipur Declaration of December 2017 from the Seventh International Conference on Peace and Nonviolent Action organised by the Jains, we called for the recognition of the importance of this issue by the peace movement. But the point is this: at the moment, in international affairs, we have complete anarchy, we have nations' intelligence services lying about each other, planting fake news, organising false flag incidents and wars, and we the people haven't got a clue what's really going on. We have my own country, the UK, accusing Russia of undertaking poisoning attacks on the streets of Salisbury but without any actual concrete scientific proven evidence. This is why I and several colleagues involved in the work of the World Intellectual Forum have recently signed a statement calling for a new International Treaty of Cyber-Peace and stated that just as people have been campaigning to rid the world of all nuclear, biological, and chemical weapons, we also believe, as philosophers and intellectuals, that the new sphere of warfare is now cyber-warfare, information war and covert propaganda, and cyber-espionage—and that to establish true peace between nations, we need to devise new treaties and new laws outlawing all such manifestations of ill will and short-term egoistical self-advantage of one nation against another. It has been estimated by experts that 80 per cent of the expenditure of the world's military intelligence budgets now goes on fake news stories, Internet monitoring, hackings, and cyber-destabilisations, including planting worms and generally trying to disrupt the intellectual life of your 'enemy.' Dr. Swaminadhan was gracious to sign this treaty amongst with other esteemed colleagues.

As intellectuals, we have a duty to insist on truth as the only possible basis for a new world order based on peace. It is as if we have been led into a post-truth world, where the key question is no longer 'what is true?' but rather 'who has the power and might here?' and as intellectuals, we have a duty to resist this degradation of human values. Politicians have shown themselves capable of corruption again and again. I personally do not care which World Parliament or government system comes into place as long as there is respect for different cultures, different religions, different philosophies of life, and different social classes, and as long as members of the World Parliament are sworn by solemn oath to *tell the truth* on all matters of public debate and official business in the house. Once they lie, they automatically lose office, and a new election is triggered for an honest person to replace them. Any new world government proposal that comes along must, in future, include this nonlying oath for the members of the World Parliament to gain my considered support. I call it the Parliamentary Duty of Veracity Bill, and I have drafted the text of such a bill suitable for the UK Parliament, where I have chaired over thirty-five seminars on peace and ethics over the years. It could be adapted for use by any future World Parliament.

Let me conclude by thanking Dr. Swaminadhan immensely for his thoughtful effort in putting together this book and saying that, I would like in a future edition, it would be most helpful if he could include a description of how his proposal differs, in detail, from those of the World Parliament and Constitution Association, and also from those of Dr. Igor Kondrashin and his United States of the Earth proposals, as well as those of other organisations and proposals for world federal government that have surfaced previously in the last few years. There are several academic centres for the study of federalism in Europe, Australia, India, and the USA, and perhaps a copy of this excellent book can be sent to them, with a suggestion that we all participate in an international online cyber conference to bring together leading federalist scholars to consider Dr. Swaminadhan's ideas in contrast other similar proposals. Let us organise this under the aegis of the World Intellectual Forum, which can then be fulfilling its own proper contribution to this mighty task.

I have one further stipulation—most governments are born through violence and warfare. If and when a world government finally comes into being, it also must be born through nonviolence, persuasion, and the power of reason alone, as Deganawidah brought the five civilised tribes into one concord. As Kant said, international federation is the logical way to solve international wars, and yet here we are, still waiting. The age of the enlightenment is surely taking a long time to catch on, and meanwhile, the nations of the world go on with their bombing, false propagandas, and uncivil wars . . . We don't have a minute to lose in our deliberations, for as Dr. Swaminadhan points out: 'On 25 January 2018, the Bulletin of the Atomic Scientists decided to reduce the symbolic time before the End of the world for another half a minute. Now only two symbolic minutes are left.' Whichever form of world government eventually emerges, if indeed it does in our lifetimes, I am sure there is still going to be a critical role for the work of intellectuals in analysing, comparing, and critiquing the best way forward. But everywhere in the world, intellectuals are under attack, and freedom of speech, freedom of thought, and freedom of assembly are sometimes denied, especially to our younger generations. We all thought the Internet would bring us freedom, but it might also be bringing us a dumbing down of thought. I hope in a future edition of this book, Dr. Swaminadhan will also remember to think of a way to build in further checks and balances to ensure that the WIF can play a monitoring role on behalf of the emerging world government structures to ensure that the rights and duties of intellectuals are respected the world over, and freedom of thought and speech and freedom of research and theorising are also respected and guaranteed by world law. Thank you, Dr. Swaminadhan, for your courageous work in publishing this timely book and for chairing the World Intellectual Forum so effectively through its formative stages.

Dr. Thomas Clough Daffern
Director, International Institute of Peace Studies and Global Philosophy World Intellectual Forum Global Regional Director (France, Europe), Paris

(Courtesy: Sri Ramanuja Mission Trust, Chennai)

PREFACE

The world has seen much havoc, misery, heavy loss of life, and destruction during the First and Second World Wars. First World War was a global war originating in Europe that lasted from July 28, 1914, to November 11, 1918. It was an international conflict that engulfed most of the nations of Europe along with Russia, the United States, the Middle East, and other regions. The war pitted the Central Powers— mainly, Germany, Austria-Hungary, and Turkey—against the Allies—mainly, France, Great Britain, Russia, Italy, Japan, and, from 1917, the United States. It ended with the defeat of the Central Powers. The war was unprecedented in terms of the slaughter, carnage, and destruction. The Second World War was a conflict that involved virtually every part of the world during the years 1939–45. The war was mainly between the Axis powers—Germany, Italy, and Japan—and the Allies—France, Great Britain, the United States, the Soviet Union, and, to a lesser extent, China. The war was in many respects a continuation, after an uneasy twenty-year hiatus, of the disputes left unsettled by World War I. World War II was the bloodiest conflict as well as the largest war in history.

(Courtesy: World Philosophical Forum (WPF), Athens)

The United Nations Organization was created in 1945 with the objective 'to save succeeding generations from the scourge of war.' However, war preparations and wars have continued. All the disarmament conventions, commissions, studies, and resolutions of the UN have failed to stop the increase and spread of military arms for war, have failed to stop the introduction of new technologies for more destructive weapons, have failed to stop more nations from acquiring nuclear weapons, and have failed to achieve disarmament. The UN has no authority or jurisdiction to end the wars. The UN has been unable to implement actions necessary to reverse major environmental damage; no programme has been launched to develop safe, sustainable, and plentiful energy supplies from solar and hydrogen sources to replace oil and coal. The UN has taken no steps towards the introduction of a single global currency that could eliminate the manipulations and devaluations of variable currencies always to the detriment of most people. No system of global finance and credit has ever been devised for the primary purpose of serving the human needs of people everywhere on a basis of equity for all. The need for replacement of UNO seems to be justified because of its failure to solve global problems. Therefore, there is need for seeking innovative approaches for forming a new world government system as an alternative to UNO.

Even great statesmen and philosophers like Jawaharlal Nehru, Sarvepalli Radhakrishnan, Albert Einstein, Bertrand Russell, Jan Tinbergen, Ban Ki-moon, John F. Kennedy, Mikhail Gorbachev, Pope Benedict XVI, Winston Churchill—all in one way or other advocated the need for a world government. Therefore, there is wisdom in suggesting the formation of a world federal government as one of the approaches to secure the future of the planet and the humanity as a whole.

All the intellectuals and philosophers are undoubtedly concerned with the future of the humankind and the planet. Towards this end, various approaches are suggested and being pursued according to one's belief and thinking. Civil societies' efforts like Earth Federation and Provisional World Parliament, Universal State of Earth, Supreme Council of Humanity (SCH), Universal Declaration on the Illegality of Wars on the Earth, and Universal Declaration of Civil Transeducation of Earth Inhabitants and such other efforts are the tools, statements, and declarations born out of deep concern for the well-being of humanity on this globe. The above Provisional World Parliament is a democratic, nonmilitary, federal world government based on establishing peace and the solving of environmental problems. Mostly they are focusing on the gravity of world situation heading for a catastrophe of human annihilation on this globe, as nonstate actors and civil societies contributing to 'global governance.'

I have been advocating a different philosophy of approach for forming a new world government through my paper 'Formation of New World Government—an Innovative Approach,' which was presented at the WIF Global Summit 2017 organised during December 2017 at Hyderabad. My approach of the formation of the World Parliament is through proportional representation of nation's parliaments and thus avoids direct election process for its formation. All the nations and their people's representatives are involved in the formation of the World Parliament and the world government.

There are two methods of calculating the proportionality of participation of countries' members of Parliament in the World Parliament. The first method is to calculate the proportionality on the basis of the countries' share of world population as indicated in annexure 2. This method shows wide variations in the countries contribution of MPs because of their huge population differences. The second method is to calculate the proportionality on the basis of the population of the six continents and their countries (annexure 4).

The new federal world government covers the seven world continents for its governance. However, only six continents (except Antarctica) are represented in the new federal world government formation. List of continents are provided in annexure 3. This method of continental proportion of MPs makes all countries equal in participation of MPs in the World Parliament.

The advantage of this new world government over the other approaches of world governance is its enforcing authority as the supreme law of the world.

Based on this line of thinking, the structure and the constitution for a new federal world government are presented in this book.

This may hopefully ignite thinking of the philosophers, intellectuals, and world leaders regarding the significance of this proposal of new federal democratic world government in finding an alternative mechanism to replace the present United Nations Organisation (UNO).

- The Author

ACKNOWLEDGEMENT

I have drafted the structure of the new world government conforming to my approach of formation of the world government. I was consulting the available literature on the subject in this regard, and in the process, I have also gone through the material on Earth Constitution. Formation of the Earth Constitution, a blueprint to build an emerging democratic world federation, is another backup strategy advocated by Dr. Glen Martin and others if UN reform proves inadequate. Both our aims are to suggest a world democratic federal government in place of the UN when a situation arises to replace it. But the philosophies of formation of the World Parliament and the world government defer.

After concretising the innovative idea of formation of the World Parliament and the world government, the remaining operative part including supportive 'organs' seems to be common for our both approaches. Therefore, I felt that instead of 'reinventing the wheel,' I may use some of the material of the Earth Constitution regarding the world government and the supportive 'organs' with suitable modifications and due acknowledgement while drafting 'the New Federal World Constitution' for the proposed 'the New Federal Democratic World Government.' I got clearance from Dr. Glen Martin in this regard. This is to acknowledge his liberal and accommodative gesture.

I thank *Dr. Thomas Clough Daffern,* director, International Institute of Peace Studies and Global Philosophy, and World Intellectual Forum Global regional director (France, Europe), Paris, for providing excellent foreword for the book.

I would recall and acknowledge the unwavering support rendered to my idea of world government by late professor *Harry Friedmann,* a former member of World Intellectual Forum (WIF).

My grateful thanks are due to *Professor S. A. R. P. V. Chaturvedi,* global co-chair, World Intellectual Forum (WIF), Hyderabad, India, for his valuable support.

I would also like to place on record my thanks to all those extended assistance in writing this book, especially *Dr. D. Suresh,* global director-general, World

Intellectual Forum (WIF), Hyderabad. My wife, *Mrs. D. Krishna Kumari,* needs special mention for her patience and encouragement throughout.

I thank Sri J. Anirudh Reddy and Sri K. Tarun Reddy—students of JNIAS School of Planning and Architecture (JNIAS-SPA), Hyderabad—for designing the cover page and converting the images to proper format. I thank Mr. D. Hari Babu, computer assistant who neatly typed the manuscript.

I acknowledge good work done by the Xlibris Publishers in publishing the book reflecting all their publishing skills.

- **The Author**

MESSAGES

DR. MANMOHAN SINGH, FORMER PRIME MINISTER OF INDIA

Dated: 31.10.2018

Dr. Manmohan Singh
manmohan@gov.in

Dear Dr. Swaminadhan,

Many thanks for your email message of 22nd October, 2018 informing that you are publishing a book titled *The New World Government—Structure and the Constitution*. The World is faced with a large number of challenges which require a collective, cooperative approach for their solutions. Unfortunately, the narrow minded nationalistic approach is now having an upper hand. I, therefore, write to send you my best wishes for the publication of your new book.

With kind regards,

Dr. Manmohan Singh
Former Prime Minister of India

THE NEW WORLD GOVERNMENT

Courtesy: The world Philosophical Forum(WPF), Athens

STRUCTURE

THE NEW WORLD GOVERNMENT STRUCTURE

BACKGROUND

The contemporary national and international scenarios in socioeconomic, political, ethnic, and cultural domains are throwing up many issues, problems, and challenges relating to development, environment, human rights, human security, communal harmony, peaceful coexistence amongst nations, and world peace and security. Existing global institutions are proving to be wanting in their structures and authorities in solving these problems. Alternatively, a new global independent organisation with enforcing authority is needed to act upon and solve these issues. The need for replacement of UNO seems to be justified because of (1) failure to solve global problems; (2) defects in organization; and (3) the UN Charter cannot be amended. Therefore, there is ample scope for evolving an innovative approach for forming a new world government system as an alternative to UNO.

The Global Summit 2017, organised during December 2017 at Hyderabad, India, by the World Intellectual Forum (WIF) with the main theme 'Contemporary World Peace and Security and the Threat of Third World War,' took note of the deteriorating conditions of the contemporary world peace and security and the imminent threat of third world war, issued a declaration (and issued a Global Summit 2017 declaration: https://drive.google.com/file/d/1T68YqWjByKSRWkTWNDE_rlE65afvqwHN/view?usp=sharing), which, inter alia, urges

(Courtesy: World Intellectual Forum (WIF)

'With regard to such a need for "An Innovative System of Government" to overcome the deficiencies of the present system of World Governance, based on the discussions that took place at the Global Summit 2017 on the concept paper presented on "Formation of New World Government—an Innovative Approach" (https://drive.google.com/file/d/0B6XQmtWYDSfOYVN5ajNlbzRzc1U/ view?usp=sharing), it was agreed that the paper may be circulated widely to all reputed organizations and institutions working in the area of World Peace and Security and after obtaining their comments/suggestions a final draft should be prepared and circulated to the National Governments and the General Assembly of the United Nations.' Action was taken accordingly by the World Intellectual Forum.

The World Intellectual Forum (WIF), having again seriously seized with the issues of (https://drive.google.com/file/d/1CR6QYyPwjVj2j-AkNkOYlsfBgHU-NXOw/view?usp=sharing) threats to global contemporary peace and security, issued further the WIF Global Appeal, dated May 1, 2018, to all the national governments and the global governance systems which, inter alia, reiterated that if the (https://drive.google.com/file/d/1Fp8CyCQHVMHiaJPWkY7Cmvlj0We0 feak/view?usp=sharing) nations failed to act on their moral duties, then we urge the evolution of an innovative approach for an alternate world government system with recognized authority to restore peace, security, and tranquillity on the globe and prevent the possibility of world wars. In this context, the concept paper on 'Formation of New World Government—an Innovative Approach' may be given due consideration by the national governments.

The proposal for the formation of a new world government based on the above concept paper is presented.

IDEA OF A NEW WORLD GOVERNMENT

'World government' refers to the idea of all humankind united under one common political authority. Critics of world government have offered three main objections relating to its feasibility, desirability, and necessity of establishing a common global political authority. First, they say that world government is infeasible; ideas of world government constitute exercises in utopian thinking and are utterly impractical as a goal for human political organization. Second, even if world government were shown to be a feasible political idea, it may be an undesirable one. It is due to the potential power and oppressiveness of a global political authority. Third, contemporary liberal theorists argue mainly that world government with supreme legislative, executive, adjudicative, and enforcement powers is largely unnecessary to solve problems such as war, global poverty, and environmental catastrophe. World government to conceive is neither necessary nor sufficient to achieve the aims of a liberal agenda.

Proponents of world government offer distinct reasons for why it is an ideal of political organization and see world government as the definitive solution to old and new human problems such as war and the development of weapons of mass destruction, global poverty and inequality, and environmental degradation.

The nineteenth and twentieth centuries witnessed revivals of proposals for world government that were fuelled by positive developments—such as technological progress in travel and communications that enabled rapid economic globalization, as well as negative developments, such as the devastating impact of wars fought with modern technology.

After the atomic bombings of Hiroshima and Nagasaki, atomic scientists lobbied for the international control of atomic energy as a main function of world federalist government. Albert Einstein wrote in 1946 that technological developments had shrunk the planet through increased economic interdependence and mutual vulnerability through weapons of mass destruction. To secure peace, Einstein asserted, 'A world government must be created which is able to solve conflicts between nations by judicial decision. This government must be based on a clear-cut constitution which is approved by the governments and nations and which gives it the sole disposition of offensive weapons.'

WORLD (GLOBAL) GOVERNANCE

'World governance' is a term that is used by people who may reject the concept of genuine world government. The concept of world governance generally do not propose a World Parliament elected by and responsible to world citizens, do not propose a world administration given executive authority and responsible to an elected World Parliament, and do not propose a world court system that functions in the context of world laws adopted by a responsible world legislature.

Civil societies' efforts like Earth Federation and Provisional World Parliament, Universal State of Earth, Supreme Council of Humanity (SCH), Universal Declaration on the Illegality of Wars on the Earth, and Universal Declaration of Civil Transeducation of Earth Inhabitants and such other efforts are the tools, statements, and declarations born out of deep concern for the well-being of humanity on this globe. The above Provisional World Parliament is a democratic, nonmilitary, federal world government based on establishing peace and the solving of environmental problems. The Constitution is not generally accepted by the population of the earth, and since it does not have institutional mechanisms to enforce itself as the supreme law for the earth, this places its status in a very interesting 'in-between.'

Mostly they are aiming at transformation of human mind and attitude through focusing on the gravity of world situation heading for a catastrophe of human annihilation on this globe as nonstate actors and civil societies contributing to 'global governance.'

GLOBAL GOVERNANCE VERSUS WORLD GOVERNMENT

While the idea of world government has experienced an intellectual resurgence in the recent years, it coexists with the concept of 'global governance,' which highlights the increasing agency of global civil society and nonstate actors with decentralized modes of achieving similar functions of government. The question is whether global governance without world government in contemporary world conditions can really deliver the goods of global security, universal human rights, social justice, and environmental protection. That has made the idea of world government a persistent human aspiration.

Courtesy: World Intellectual Forum(WIF)

STRUCTURE OF THE NEW WORLD GOVERNMENT

Taking a cue from liberal theories envisioning the need for authoritative international and global institutions that modify the powers and prerogatives traditionally attributed to the sovereign states, an innovative approach for the formation of a democratic, presidential, and federal form of world government is proposed.

1. THE WORLD PARLIAMENT

(a)		The World Parliament is formed through proportional representation of nation's parliaments. There are two methods of calculating the proportionality of participation of countries' members of Parliament in the World Parliament. The first method is to calculate the proportionality on the basis of the countries' share of world population as indicated in annexure 2. This method shows wide variations in the countries' contribution of MPs because of their huge population differences. The new world government covers the seven world continents for its governance. However, only six continents (except Antarctica) are represented in the in new world government formation. The second method is to calculate the proportionality on the basis of the six continents and their countries (annexure 4). This method of continental proportion of MPs makes all countries equal in participation of MPs in the World Parliament.
(b)		The World Parliament comprises two houses: upper house (Elders' House) and lower house.
	(i)	The upper house is presided over by the chairman assisted by five deputy chairmen representing the six (leaving Antarctica) continental areas and to be elected by the house.
	(ii)	The lower house is presided over by the speaker assisted by five deputy speakers representing the six continental areas. They will be elected by the lower house.

(c)		The World Parliament will have 'treasury benches.' The treasury benches will be composed of the members of Parliament of nation's parliament contributed by either one of the methods indicated under item 1(a) above.
(d)		The World Parliament will have 'opposition benches' as well to play a 'watchdog' role with proportional representation of nations' opposition parties as indicated in annexure 2 and 4.
(e)		Thus, the World Parliament will not get involved in any 'election process' on its own.
(f)		The power sharing between upper house and the lower house of the World Parliament will be worked out by a standing committee of World Parliament (both the houses represented).
(g)		The tenure of the World Parliament will be five years at a time.
(h)		This will form the legislative wing of the world government.
	(iii)	An illustrative example of one-thousand-strong New World Parliament based on the two methods of calculating the proportionality of presentation of MPs to World Parliament are shown in annexures 2 and 4.

2. THE WORLD CONSTITUTION

(i)		The world government will have a World Constitution.
(ii)		It provides for legislative, executive, and judiciary wings of governance.
(iii)		Justice, liberty, equality, and fraternity will form the basis for framing the constitution. It means the constitution guaranties to all the nations and their peoples:
	(a)	justice - socioeconomic and political
	(b)	liberty - of thought, expression, belief, and faith
	(c)	equality - of opportunity and status
	(d)	fraternity - promote amongst all nations unity and integrity, assuring freedom and dignity of people and nations.
(iv)		The citizens of the nations forming the world federal government will automatically become the *world citizens*.
(v)		The World Constitution will come in to force from the date of approval by the World Parliament.

3. THE NEW WORLD GOVERNMENT

(a)	The new world government will be a democratic, presidential, and federal form of government.
(b)	One president and five vice presidents will form the heads of world government.
(c)	Sixty cabinet ministers headed by the president and vice presidents will form the cabinet. This will be the executive wing of the world government.
(d)	The tenure of the world government will be five years at a time.

4. WORLD SUPREME COURT

The world government will have an independent World Supreme Court situated in the primary capital city, and five benches of World Supreme Court will be installed in the other five secondary world capital cities or elsewhere. This forms the judiciary wing of the world government.

5. NATIONAL SUPREME COURTS AND JUDICIARY

Each nation will have its own supreme courts, high courts, and the subordinate judiciary.

6. CAPITAL CITIES

With a view to have wider dispersal of world capital cities, six world capital cities—one primary and five secondary world capital cities—will be established in six continental areas. The proposed world capital cities and their location in the world map is shown in annexure 5.

7. GLOBAL CURRENCY

The world government will have a global currency.

8. WORLD ARMY

The world government will have a World Army to intervene in wars or conflicts between countries and to take care of defence in case of interplanetary conflicts.

9. NATIONAL ARMY

Each nation will prune its existing national army strength and contribute to the World Army. They may continue to maintain their security and intelligence structures.

10. WORLD POLICE SYSTEM

To maintain law and order, the world government will have a World Police System.

11. WORLD INTELLIGENCE AGENCY

The world government will maintain a World Intelligence Agency for intelligence and security.

12. THE EXISTING WORLD INSTITUTIONS

The World Bank (WB), International Monitory Fund (IMF), World Health Organisation (WHO), World Food Organisation (WFO), the UNESCO, and other similar world bodies will continue to exist under the proposed world government.

13. UN AND OTHER BODIES

Naturally, the United Nations Organisation (UNO) with its General Assembly and Security Council will cease to exist after the new world government is formed. The other UN-affiliated bodies except those listed under clause 12 above will also cease to exist.

14. (A) WORLD CULTURAL COUNCIL AND WORLD CULTURAL CENTRE

The World Cultural Centre will provide full-fledged infrastructure for study, research, and cultural activities, and it will act as a 'melting pot' of east-west-south-north ancient knowledge, wisdom, languages, and cultures for the well-being of humanity. It will be governed by a World Cultural Council (WCC). The council will be represented on a linguistic basis, with each language of the world represented, and will be made up of intellectuals, writers, poets, philologists, and philosophers. About four billion of the earth's 6.5 billion people, or over 60 per cent of the earth's population, speak one of the main thirty languages as their native tongue: Chinese (Mandarin), Hindi, Spanish, English, Arabic, Portuguese, Bengali, Russian, Japanese, German, Panjabi, Javanese, Korean, Vietnamese, Telugu, Marathi, Tamil, French, Urdu, Italian, Turkish, Persian, Gujarati, Polish, Ukrainian, Malayalam, Kannada, Oriya, Burmese, and Thai. Adding another of the two hundred most populous languages on the planet and we would have about four hundred delegates representing these languages.

(Courtesy: UNO)

Discussions, debates, round tables, seminars, conferences, and exhibitions on various cultures, traditions, and religious and communal unity and harmony will be held periodically. This may act as a 'think tank' on world cultures, traditions, languages, communal harmony, and human values and offer policy inputs to the world government. The World Cultural Council will be constituted by the world cabinet for a five-year term and approves adequate budget for the council and the World Cultural Centre.

B) WORLD INTERFAITH COUNCIL

Faith is the orderly fashion of any form of belief endowed with exclusive philosophy, customs, and practices. In wider sense, it accommodates all atheistic, sociocentric, and cosmocentric schools like naturalism, socialism, and scientific materialism. In brief, it is the common minimal agenda of all faiths accepting the need and their role in building a strong, serene, and peaceful earth.

The world government will support the World Interfaith Council, which inspires, educates, and mobilizes people to unite across differences and to act from their shared ethical and spiritual values in pursuit of peace. The interfaith council envisions a world free from violence, including the violence of war, poverty, oppression, and environmental devastation. To enact this vision, it commits to nurture a community in which compassion and respect foster actions that dismantle systems of violence while simultaneously creating systems of peace, justice, and ecological sustainability.

The interfaith council comprises leaders of all faiths of the world and social animators. The cabinet will constitute the interfaith council with a five-year term. Adequate budget provision will be made by the world government.

15. WORLD GOVERNANCE CONSTITUENTS

A) NONSTATE ACTORS AND CIVIL SOCIETIES

The world government will recognise the good efforts made by the civil societies and nonstate actors, and it will interact with them through a suitable interface mechanism.

B) THE FOURTH ESTATE

The world government will also enlist the support of the fourth estate for effective governance. The interface mechanism meant for global governance will include the fourth estate also.

C) INTERFACE MECHANISM

The interface mechanism will be in the form of a 'global think tank' comprising members of world governance constituents and the fourth estate, which will provide the policy inputs and counselling to the world government.

16. FEATURES OF THE NEW WORLD GOVERNMENT

The world government will stand out as an effective organisation offering definitive solution to old and new human problems such as war and the development of weapons of mass destruction, global poverty and inequality, and environmental degradation and work towards nuclear nonproliferation and disarmament. The proposed world government will also satisfy the requirements of freedom—the world will be poised to break free of both capitalism and imperialism; unity—the world can be united, overcoming both the east-west and the north-south divides; world peace—the world can begin disarmament, replacing the war system with a world peace system; human rights—economic and political institutions will be put in place to protect human rights worldwide; and sustainability—institutions will be put in place to ensure a sustainable world system. Participation of all nations of world is ensured in the operation of the world government.

17. THE STRUCTURE OF THE NEW WORLD GOVERNMENT IS SHOWN IN ANNEXURE 1.

ANNEXURE I

The New World Government
The World Parliament

FIG. 1 STRUCTURE OF THE NEW WORLD GOVERNMENT

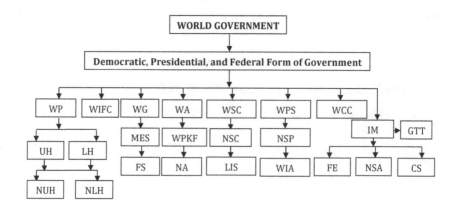

INDEX

WP	World Parliament	IM	Interface Mechanism
WG	World Government	NSC	National Supreme Courts
WA	World Army	WPS	World Police System
WSC	World Supreme Court	FS	Federal Structure (world and nation states)
WIFC	World Interfaith Council	NA	National Armies
MES	Ministers and Executive Structure	LIS	Local Judiciary Structure
WPKF	World Peacekeeping Force	NSP	Nation State Police
NSA	Nonstate Actors	FE	Fourth Estate
GTT	Global Think Tank	CS	Civil Societies
WCC	World Cultural Council	WIA	World Intelligence Agency
UH	Upper House	LH	Lower House
NUH	National Upper House	NLH	National Lower House

ANNEXURE II

THE NEW WORLD GOVERNMENT
THE WORLD PARLIAMENT

REPRESENTATION OF COUNTRIES TO THE WORLD PARLIAMENT PROPORTIONAL TO THEIR POPULATION

S. No.	Country (or dependency)	Population (2018)	World Population Share	Lower House (1000 MPs)		Upper House (500 MPs)	
				(Treasury Benches) Proportional to World Share Population	(Opposition Benches) (10% of Treasury Benches)	(Treasury Benches) Proportional to World Share Population	(Opposition Benches) (10% of Treasury Benches)
1	China	1,415,045,928	18.54%	**185**	18	93	9
2	India	1,354,051,854	17.74%	177	17	89	9
3	U.S.	326,766,748	4.28%	42	4	21	2
4	Indonesia	266,794,980	3.50%	35	4	18	2

S. No.	Country (or dependency)	Population (2018)	World Population Share	Lower House (1000 MPs)		Upper House (500 MPs)	
				(Treasury Benches) Proportional to World Share Population	(Opposition Benches) (10% of Treasury Benches)	(Treasury Benches) Proportional to World Share Population	(Opposition Benches) (10% of Treasury Benches)
5	Brazil	210,867,954	2.76%	27	3	14	2
6	Pakistan	200,813,818	2.63%	26	3	13	2
7	Nigeria	195,875,237	2.57%	25	3	13	2
8	Bangladesh	166,368,149	2.18%	21	2	11	1
9	Russia	143,964,709	1.89%	18	2	9	1
10	Mexico	130,759,074	1.71%	17	2	9	1
11	Japan	127,185,332	1.67%	16	2	8	1
12	Ethiopia	107,534,882	1.41%	14	1	7	1
13	Philippines	106,512,074	1.40%	14	1	7	1
14	Egypt	99,375,741	1.30%	13	1	7	1
15	Viet Nam	96,491,146	1.26%	12	1	6	1
16	DR Congo	84,004,989	1.10%	11	1	6	1
17	Germany	82,293,457	1.08%	10	1	5	1
18	Iran	82,011,735	1.07%	10	1	5	1
19	Turkey	81,916,871	1.07%	10	1	5	1
20	Thailand	69,183,173	0.91%	9	1	5	1
21	UK	66,573,504	0.87%	8	1	4	1
22	France	65,233,271	0.85%	8	1	4	1
23	Italy	59,290,969	0.78%	7	1	4	1
24	Tanzania	59,091,392	0.77%	7	1	4	1
25	South Africa	57,398,421	0.75%	7	1	4	1
26	Myanmar	53,855,735	0.71%	7	1	4	1
27	South Korea	51,164,435	0.67%	6	1	3	1
28	Kenya	50,950,879	0.67%	6	1	3	1
29	Colombia	49,464,683	0.65%	6	1	3	1
30	Spain	46,397,452	0.61%	6	1	3	1
31	Argentina	44,688,864	0.59%	5	1	3	1
32	Uganda	44,270,563	0.58%	5	1	3	1
33	Ukraine	44,009,214	0.58%	5	1	3	1
34	Algeria	42,008,054	0.55%	5	1	3	1

S. No.	Country (or dependency)	Population (2018)	World Population Share	Lower House (1000 MPs)		Upper House (500 MPs)	
				(Treasury Benches) Proportional to World Share Population	(Opposition Benches) (10% of Treasury Benches)	(Treasury Benches) Proportional to World Share Population	(Opposition Benches) (10% of Treasury Benches)
35	Sudan	41,511,526	0.54%	5	1	3	1
36	Iraq	39,339,753	0.52%	5	1	3	1
37	Poland	38,104,832	0.50%	5	1	3	1
38	Canada	36,953,765	0.48%	4	1	2	1
39	Afghanistan	36,373,176	0.48%	4	1	2	1
40	Morocco	36,191,805	0.47%	4	1	2	1
41	Saudi Arabia	33,554,343	0.44%	4	1	2	1
42	Peru	32,551,815	0.43%	4	1	2	1
43	Venezuela	32,381,221	0.42%	4	1	2	1
44	Uzbekistan	32,364,996	0.42%	4	1	2	1
45	Malaysia	32,042,458	0.42%	4	1	2	1
46	Angola	30,774,205	0.40%	4	1	2	1
47	Mozambique	30,528,673	0.40%	4	1	2	1
48	Nepal	29,624,035	0.39%	3	1	2	1
49	Ghana	29,463,643	0.39%	3	1	2	1
50	Yemen	28,915,284	0.38%	3	1	2	1
51	Madagascar	26,262,810	0.34%	3	1	2	1
52	North Korea	25,610,672	0.34%	3	1	2	1
53	Côte d'Ivoire	24,905,843	0.33%	3	1	2	1
54	Australia	24,772,247	0.32%	3	1	2	1
55	Cameroon	24,678,234	0.32%	3	1	2	1
56	Taiwan	23,694,089	0.31%	3	1	2	1
57	Niger	22,311,375	0.29%	2	1	1	1
58	Sri Lanka	20,950,041	0.27%	2	1	1	1
59	Burkina Faso	19,751,651	0.26%	2	1	1	1
60	Romania	19,580,634	0.26%	2	1	1	1
61	Malawi	19,164,728	0.25%	2	1	1	1
62	Mali	19,107,706	0.25%	2	1	1	1
63	Kazakhstan	18,403,860	0.24%	2	1	1	1
64	Syria	18,284,407	0.24%	2	1	1	1

S. No.	Country (or dependency)	Population (2018)	World Population Share	Lower House (1000 MPs)		Upper House (500 MPs)	
				(Treasury Benches) Proportional to World Share Population	(Opposition Benches) (10% of Treasury Benches)	(Treasury Benches) Proportional to World Share Population	(Opposition Benches) (10% of Treasury Benches)
65	Chile	18,197,209	0.24%	2	1	1	1
66	Zambia	17,609,178	0.23%	2	1	1	1
67	Guatemala	17,245,346	0.23%	2	1	1	1
68	Netherlands	17,084,459	0.22%	2	1	1	1
69	Zimbabwe	16,913,261	0.22%	2	1	1	1
70	Ecuador	16,863,425	0.22%	2	1	1	1
71	Senegal	16,294,270	0.21%	2	1	1	1
72	Cambodia	16,245,729	0.21%	2	1	1	1
73	Chad	15,353,184	0.20%	2	1	1	1
74	Somalia	15,181,925	0.20%	2	1	1	1
75	Guinea	13,052,608	0.17%	1	1	1	1
76	South Sudan	12,919,053	0.17%	1	1	1	1
77	Rwanda	12,501,156	0.16%	1	1	1	1
78	Tunisia	11,659,174	0.15%	1	1	1	1
79	Belgium	11,498,519	0.15%	1	1	1	1
80	Cuba	11,489,082	0.15%	1	1	1	1
81	Benin	11,485,674	0.15%	1	1	1	1
82	Burundi	11,216,450	0.15%	1	1	1	1
83	Bolivia	11,215,674	0.15%	1	1	1	1
84	Greece	11,142,161	0.15%	1	1	1	1
85	Haiti	11,112,945	0.15%	1	1	1	1
86	Dominican Republic	10,882,996	0.14%	1	1	1	1
87	Czech Republic	10,625,250	0.14%	1	1	1	1
88	Portugal	10,291,196	0.13%	1	1	1	1
89	Sweden	9,982,709	0.13%	1	1	1	1
90	Azerbaijan	9,923,914	0.13%	1	1	1	1
91	Jordan	9,903,802	0.13%	1	1	1	1
92	Hungary	9,688,847	0.13%	1	1	1	1

S. No.	Country (or dependency)	Population (2018)	World Population Share	Lower House (1000 MPs)		Upper House (500 MPs)	
				(Treasury Benches) Proportional to World Share Population	(Opposition Benches) (10% of Treasury Benches)	(Treasury Benches) Proportional to World Share Population	(Opposition Benches) (10% of Treasury Benches)
93	United Arab Emirates	9,541,615	0.13%	1	1	1	1
94	Belarus	9,452,113	0.12%	1	1	1	1
95	Honduras	9,417,167	0.12%	1	1	1	1
96	Tajikistan	9,107,211	0.12%	1	1	1	1
97	Serbia	8,762,027	0.11%	1	1	1	1
98	Austria	8,751,820	0.11%	1	1	1	1
99	Switzerland	8,544,034	0.11%	1	1	1	1
100	Israel	8,452,841	0.11%	1	1	1	1
101	Papua New Guinea	8,418,346	0.11%	1	1	1	1
102	Togo	7,990,926	0.10%	1	1	1	1
103	Sierra Leone	7,719,729	0.10%	1	1	1	1
104	Hong Kong	7,428,887	0.10%	1	1	1	1
105	Bulgaria	7,036,848	0.09%	1	1	1	1
106	Laos	6,961,210	0.09%	1	1	1	1
107	Paraguay	6,896,908	0.09%	1	1	1	1
108	Libya	6,470,956	0.08%	1	1	1	1
109	El Salvador	6,411,558	0.08%	1	1	1	1
110	Nicaragua	6,284,757	0.08%	1	1	1	1
111	Kyrgyzstan	6,132,932	0.08%	1	1	1	1
112	Lebanon	6,093,509	0.08%	1	1	1	1
113	Turkmenistan	5,851,466	0.08%	1	1	1	1
114	Singapore	5,791,901	0.08%	1	1	1	1
115	Denmark	5,754,356	0.08%	1	1	1	1
116	Finland	5,542,517	0.07%	1	1	1	1
117	Slovakia	5,449,816	0.07%	1	1	1	1
118	Congo	5,399,895	0.07%	1	1	1	1
119	Norway	5,353,363	0.07%	1	1	1	1
120	Eritrea	5,187,948	0.07%	1	1	1	1

S. No.	Country (or dependency)	Population (2018)	World Population Share	Lower House (1000 MPs)		Upper House (500 MPs)	
				(Treasury Benches) Proportional to World Share Population	(Opposition Benches) (10% of Treasury Benches)	(Treasury Benches) Proportional to World Share Population	(Opposition Benches) (10% of Treasury Benches)
121	State of Palestine	5,052,776	0.07%	1	1	1	1
122	Costa Rica	4,953,199	0.06%	1	1	1	1
123	Liberia	4,853,516	0.06%	1	1	1	1
124	Oman	4,829,946	0.06%	1	1	1	1
125	Ireland	4,803,748	0.06%	1	1	1	1
126	New Zealand	4,749,598	0.06%	1	1	1	1
127	Central African Republic	4,737,423	0.06%	1	1	1	1
128	Mauritania	4,540,068	0.06%	1	1	1	1
129	Kuwait	4,197,128	0.05%	1	1	1	1
130	Croatia	4,164,783	0.05%	1	1	1	1
131	Panama	4,162,618	0.05%	1	1	1	1
132	Moldova	4,041,065	0.05%	1	1	1	1
133	Georgia	3,907,131	0.05%	1	1	1	1
134	Puerto Rico	3,659,007	0.05%	1	1	1	1
135	Bosnia and Herzegovina	3,503,554	0.05%	1	1	1	1
136	Uruguay	3,469,551	0.05%	1	1	1	1
137	Mongolia	3,121,772	0.04%	1	1	1	1
138	Albania	2,934,363	0.04%	1	1	1	1
139	Armenia	2,934,152	0.04%	1	1	1	1
140	Jamaica	2,898,677	0.04%	1	1	1	1
141	Lithuania	2,876,475	0.04%	1	1	1	1
142	Qatar	2,694,849	0.04%	1	1	1	1
143	Namibia	2,587,801	0.03%	1	1	1	1
144	Botswana	2,333,201	0.03%	1	1	1	1
145	Lesotho	2,263,010	0.03%	1	1	1	1
146	Gambia	2,163,765	0.03%	1	1	1	1
147	TFYR Macedonia	2,085,051	0.03%	1	1	1	1

S. No.	Country (or dependency)	Population (2018)	World Population Share	Lower House (1000 MPs)		Upper House (500 MPs)	
				(Treasury Benches) Proportional to World Share Population	(Opposition Benches) (10% of Treasury Benches)	(Treasury Benches) Proportional to World Share Population	(Opposition Benches) (10% of Treasury Benches)
148	Slovenia	2,081,260	0.03%	1	1	1	1
149	Gabon	2,067,561	0.03%	1	1	1	1
150	Latvia	1,929,938	0.03%	1	1	1	1
151	Guinea-Bissau	1,907,268	0.02%	1	1	1	1
152	Bahrain	1,566,993	0.02%	1	1	1	1
153	Swaziland	1,391,385	0.02%	1	1	1	1
154	Trinidad and Tobago	1,372,598	0.02%	1	1	1	1
155	Timor-Leste	1,324,094	0.02%	1	1	1	1
156	Equatorial Guinea	1,313,894	0.02%	1	1	1	1
157	Estonia	1,306,788	0.02%	1	1	1	1
158	Mauritius	1,268,315	0.02%	1	1	1	1
159	Cyprus	1,189,085	0.02%	1	1	1	1
160	Djibouti	971,408	0.01%	1	1	1	1
161	Fiji	912,241	0.01%	1	1	1	1
162	Réunion	883,247	0.01%	1	1	1	1
163	Comoros	832,347	0.01%	1	1	1	1
164	Bhutan	817,054	0.01%	1	1	1	1
165	Guyana	782,225	0.01%	1	1	1	1
166	Macao	632,418	0.01%	1	1	1	1
167	Montenegro	629,219	0.01%	1	1	1	1
168	Solomon Islands	623,281	0.01%	1	1	1	1
169	Luxembourg	590,321	0.01%	1	1	1	1
170	Suriname	568,301	0.01%	1	1	1	1
171	Western Sahara	567,421	0.01%	1	1	1	1
172	Cabo Verde	553,335	0.01%	1	1	1	1
173	Guadeloupe	449,173	0.01%	1	1	1	1
174	Maldives	444,259	0.01%	1	1	1	1

S. No.	Country (or dependency)	Population (2018)	World Population Share	Lower House (1000 MPs)		Upper House (500 MPs)	
				(Treasury Benches) Proportional to World Share Population	(Opposition Benches) (10% of Treasury Benches)	(Treasury Benches) Proportional to World Share Population	(Opposition Benches) (10% of Treasury Benches)
175	Brunei	434,076	0.01%	1	1	1	1
176	Malta	432,089	0.01%	1	1	1	1
177	Bahamas	399,285	0.01%	1	1	1	1
178	Martinique	385,065	0.01%	1	1	1	1
179	Belize	382,444	0.01%	1	1	1	1
180	Iceland	337,780	0.00%	1	1	1	1
181	French Guiana	289,763	0.00%	1	1	1	1
182	Barbados	286,388	0.00%	1	1	1	1
183	French Polynesia	285,859	0.00%	1	1	1	1
184	Vanuatu	282,117	0.00%	1	1	1	1
185	New Caledonia	279,821	0.00%	1	1	1	1
186	Mayotte	259,682	0.00%	1	1	1	1
187	Sao Tome and Principe	208,818	0.00%	1	1	1	1
188	Samoa	197,695	0.00%	1	1	1	1
189	Saint Lucia	179,667	0.00%	1	1	1	1
190	Channel Islands	166,083	0.00%	1	1	1	1
191	Guam	165,718	0.00%	1	1	1	1
192	Curaçao	161,577	0.00%	1	1	1	1
193	Kiribati	118,414	0.00%	1	1	1	1
194	St. Vincent and Grenadines	110,200	0.00%	1	1	1	1
195	Tonga	109,008	0.00%	1	1	1	1
196	Grenada	108,339	0.00%	1	1	1	1
197	Micronesia	106,227	0.00%	1	1	1	1
198	Aruba	105,670	0.00%	1	1	1	1

S. No.	Country (or dependency)	Population (2018)	World Population Share	Lower House (1000 MPs)		Upper House (500 MPs)	
				(Treasury Benches) Proportional to World Share Population	(Opposition Benches) (10% of Treasury Benches)	(Treasury Benches) Proportional to World Share Population	(Opposition Benches) (10% of Treasury Benches)
199	U.S. Virgin Islands	104,914	0.00%	1	1	1	1
200	Antigua and Barbuda	103,050	0.00%	1	1	1	1
201	Seychelles	95,235	0.00%	1	1	1	1
202	Isle of Man	84,831	0.00%	1	1	1	1
203	Andorra	76,953	0.00%	1	1	1	1
204	Dominica	74,308	0.00%	1	1	1	1
205	Cayman Islands	62,348	0.00%	1	1	1	1
206	Bermuda	61,070	0.00%	1	1	1	1
207	Greenland	56,565	0.00%	1	1	1	1
208	Saint Kitts and Nevis	55,850	0.00%	1	1	1	1
209	American Samoa	55,679	0.00%	1	1	1	1
210	Northern Mariana Islands	55,194	0.00%	1	1	1	1
211	Marshall Islands	53,167	0.00%	1	1	1	1
212	Faeroe Islands	49,489	0.00%	1	1	1	1
213	Sint Maarten	40,552	0.00%	1	1	1	1
214	Monaco	38,897	0.00%	1	1	1	1
215	Liechtenstein	38,155	0.00%	1	1	1	1
216	Turks and Caicos	35,963	0.00%	1	1	1	1
217	Gibraltar	34,733	0.00%	1	1	1	1
218	San Marino	33,557	0.00%	1	1	1	1
219	British Virgin Islands	31,719	0.00%	1	1	1	1

S. No.	Country (or dependency)	Population (2018)	World Population Share	Lower House (1000 MPs)		Upper House (500 MPs)	
				(Treasury Benches) Proportional to World Share Population	(Opposition Benches) (10% of Treasury Benches)	(Treasury Benches) Proportional to World Share Population	(Opposition Benches) (10% of Treasury Benches)
220	Caribbean Netherlands	25,702	0.00%	1	1	1	1
221	Palau	21,964	0.00%	1	1	1	1
222	Cook Islands	17,411	0.00%	1	1	1	1
223	Anguilla	15,045	0.00%	1	1	1	1
224	Wallis and Futuna	11,683	0.00%	1	1	1	1
225	Nauru	11,312	0.00%	1	1	1	1
226	Tuvalu	11,287	0.00%	1	1	1	1
227	Saint Pierre and Miquelon	6,342	0.00%	1	1	1	1
228	Montserrat	5,203	0.00%	1	1	1	1
229	Saint Helena	4,074	0.00%	1	1	1	1
230	Falkland Islands	2,922	0.00%	1	1	1	1
231	Niue	1,624	0.00%	1	1	1	1
232	Tokelau	1,319	0.00%	1	1	1	1
233	Holy See	801	0.00%	1	1	1	1
		Total:		1064	281	624	254

* Source: Worldometers (www.Worldometers.info)

Elaboration of data by United Nations, Department of Economic and Social Affairs, Population Division. World Population Prospects: The 2017 Revision. (Medium-fertility variant).

* Only for the countries' population and their share in the world population.

(Courtesy: World Philosophical Forum (WPF), Athens)

(Courtesy: Sri Ramanuja Mission Trust, Chennai, India)

ANNEXURE III

The New World Government
The World Parliament

CONTINENTS OF THE WORLD CONSIDERED FOR THE FORMATION OF THE NEW WORLD GOVERNMENT

All the widely recognized seven continents are listed by size below, from biggest to smallest.

- **ASIA** includes fifty countries, and it is the most populated continent; 60 per cent of the total population of the earth lives here.
- **AFRICA** comprises fifty-four countries. It is the hottest continent and home of the world's largest desert, the Sahara, occupying the 25 per cent of the total area of Africa.
- **NORTH AMERICA** includes twenty-three countries led by the USA as the largest economy in the world.
- **SOUTH AMERICA** comprises twelve countries. Here is located the largest forest, the Amazon rainforest, which covers 30 per cent of South America's total area.

- **ANTARCTICA** is the coldest continent in the world completely covered with ice. There are no permanent inhabitants, except scientists maintaining research stations in Antarctica.
- **EUROPE** comprises fifty-one countries. It is the most developed economically continent, with the European Union as the biggest economic and political union in the world.
- **AUSTRALIA** includes fourteen countries. It is the least populated continent after Antarctica, only 0.3 per cent of the total earth population lives here.

Continents by area from largest to smallest

Rank	Continent	Total Area (sq. km)	Total Area (sq. mi)
1	Asia	44,579,000	17,212,000
2	Africa	30,370,000	11,730,000
3	North America	24,709,000	9,540,000
4	South America	17,840,000	6,890,000
5	Antarctica	14,000,000	5,400,000
6	Europe	10,180,000	3,930,000
7	Australia	8,600,000	3,300,000

Reference: www.countries-ofthe-world.com

ANNEXURE IV

THE NEW WORLD GOVERNMENT
THE WORLD PARLIAMENT

PROPORTIONAL REPRESENTATION OF MEMBERS OF PARLIAMENT OF COUNTRIES OF EACH CONTINENT AND THEIR CONTRIBUTION TO THE WORLD PARLIAMENT

The new federal world government covers the seven world continents for its governance. However, only six continents (except Antarctica) are represented in the formation of the New World Parliament and the new federal world government.

S. No.	Continents	Number of Countries	Lower House (1000 MPs)			Upper House (500 MPs)		
			Treasury Benches	Proportion of MPs for each Country	Opposition Benches (40% of Treasury Benches	Treasury Benches	Proportion of MPs for each Country	Opposition Benches (50% of Treasury Benches

1.	Asia	50	245	5	2	122	2	1
2.	Africa	54	265	5	2	132	2	1
3.	North America	23	113	5	2	57	2	1
4.	South America	12	59	5	2	30	2	1
5.	Europe	51	250	5	2	125	2	1
6.	Australia	14	68	5	2	34	2	1
	Total:	**204**	**1000**			**500**		

Note:

1. According to the method of calculating continental proportion of members of Parliament (MPs) to the World Parliament, each country will contribute equally five MPs for the treasury benches of the lower house and two MPs each for the opposition benches (fractions are rounded off).
2. Similarly for the upper house, two MPs for treasury benches and one MP for the opposition bench will be contributed by each country.
3. This method of continental proportion of MPs makes all countries equal in contributing of MPs to the World Parliament.

ANNEXURE V

The New World Government
The World Parliament

STATEMENT OF PROPOSED WORLD CAPITAL CITIES AND THEIR LOCATION INDICATED ON THE WORLD MAP

S. No.	Name of the Continent	World Government Capital Cities	
		Primary	Secondary
1.	North America	New York, USA	
2.	Asia		New Delhi, India
3.	Africa		Johannesburg, South Africa
4.	South America		Rio de Janeiro, Brazil
5.	Europe		London, UK
6.	Australia		Sydney, Australia
7.	Antarctica	-	-

Note: The world government capital cities are shown in red circles in the world map below.

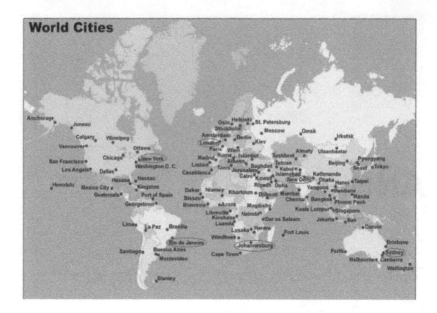

THE NEW WORLD GOVERNMENT

CONSTITUTION

PREAMBLE

Conscious that alternative to UNO, an independent world institutional mechanism empowered with supreme enforcing authority can only play an objective and independent role in finding solutions to the problems and issues of human sufferings, welfare, and development and prevention of wars and conflicts and conscious of the inescapable reality that the greatest hope for the survival of life on earth is the establishment of a democratic world government:

We, the nations of the world, have solemnly resolved to establish the federal, democratic, and presidential forum of the new world government (the new world government) and to be governed in accordance with this constitution with a view to secure to all people and nations of the world:

a) justice - socioeconomic and political;
b) liberty - of thought, expression, belief, and faith;
c) equality - of opportunity and status; and
d) fraternity - promote amongst all nations unity and integrity assuring the freedom and dignity of people and nations.

IN OUR WORLD PARLIAMENT this (date) day of (month), (year), DO HEREBY ADOPT, ENACT, AND GIVE OURSELVES THIS CONSTITUTION.

THE CONSTITUTION FOR THE NEW WORLD GOVERNMENT

ARTICLES

Article 1			**Constitution of the New World Government** The new world government will have a New World Constitution.
		1.	The New World Constitution provides for legislative, executive, and judiciary wings of governance.
		2.	Justice, liberty, equality, and fraternity will form the basis for framing the constitution. It means the constitution guaranties to all the nations and their peoples: a) justice - socioeconomic and political; b) liberty - of thought, expression, belief, and faith; c) equality - of opportunity and status; and d) fraternity - promote amongst all nations unity and integrity assuring freedom and dignity of people and nations.
		3.	The New World Constitution will come in to force from the date of approval by the World Parliament.
Article 2			**The New World Government** The new world government will be a democratic, presidential, and federal form of government. The tenure of the new world government will be five years at a time.

	Sec. A		**Broad Functions of New World Government**
		1.	To secure to all people and nations: a) justice - socioeconomic and political; b) liberty - of thought, expression, belief, and faith; c) equality - of opportunity and status; and d) fraternity - promote amongst all nations unity and integrity assuring freedom and dignity of people and nations.
		2.	To play an objective and independent role in finding solutions to the problems and issues of human sufferings, welfare, and development and prevention of wars and conflicts.
		3.	To deter nations to stop the increase and spread of military arms for war and introduction of new technologies for more destructive weapons and for acquiring nuclear weapons and encourage to work towards achieving disarmament.
		4.	To implement actions necessary to reverse major environmental damages and to sustain a good livable environment on earth.
		5.	To undertake intensive global 'crash' program to develop safe, sustainable, and plentiful energy supplies from solar and hydrogen sources to replace oil and coal.
		6.	To take steps towards the introduction of a single global currency and introduce a system of global finance and credit for the primary purpose of serving the human needs of people everywhere, on a basis of equity for all.
		7.	To devise and implement solutions to all problems that are beyond the capacity of national governments or that are now or may become of global or international concern or consequence.
		8.	To devise and implement solutions to issues, problems, and challenges relating to development, environment, human rights, human security, communal harmony, peaceful coexistence amongst nations, and world peace and security.

		9.	To enlist the cooperation and association of the nonstate actors, civil societies, and the fourth estate through a suitable interface mechanism for effective governance. The interface mechanism shall be in the form of a'global think tank' comprising of members of world governance constituents and the fourth estate, which will provide the policy inputs and counselling to the world government.
Article 3			**Organs of the New World Government** The organs of the new world government shall be
		1.	the World Parliament
		2.	the world executive
		3.	the world administration
		4.	the supportive divisions
		5.	the world judiciary
		6.	the World Army
		7.	the World Intelligence Agency
		8.	the World Police System
		9.	the interface
Article 4			**The Powers of the New World Government**
	Sec. A		The powers of the new world government to be exercised through its several organs and agencies shall comprise the following:
		1.	prevent wars and armed conflicts amongst the nations, regions, and peoples of the globe;
		2.	supervise disarmament and prevent rearmament; prohibit and eliminate the design, testing, manufacture, sale, purchase, use, and possession of weapons of mass destruction; and prohibit or regulate all lethal weapons that the World Parliament may decide;
		3.	prohibit incitement to war, hatred, genocide, and discrimination against gender, race, religion, ethnicity, language, region, and culture;
		4.	provide the means for peaceful and just solutions of disputes and conflicts amongst or between nations, peoples, and/or other components within the world government;

		5.	supervise boundary settlements and conduct plebiscites as needed;
		6.	codify world laws, including the body of international law developed prior to adoption of the World Constitution, but not inconsistent therewith, and which is approved by the World Parliament;
		7.	establish universal standards for weights, measurements, accounting, and records;
		8.	provide assistance in the event of large-scale calamities, including drought, famine, pestilence, flood, earthquake, hurricane, ecological disruptions, and other disasters;
		9	guarantee and enforce the civil liberties and the basic human rights;
		10	define standards and promote the worldwide improvement in working conditions, nutrition, health, housing, human settlements, environmental conditions, education, and economic security;
		11	regulate and supervise international transportation, communications, postal services, and migrations of people;
		12	regulate and supervise supranational trade, industry, corporations, businesses, cartels, professional services, labour supply, finances, investments, and insurance;
		13	secure and supervise the elimination of tariffs and other trade barriers amongst nations, but with provisions to prevent or minimize hardship for those previously protected by tariffs;
		14	raise the revenues and funds, by direct and/or indirect means, that are necessary for the purposes and activities of the world government;
		15	and insurance institutions designed to serve human needs; establish, issue, and regulate world currency, credit, and exchange;
		16	common heritage of humanity; protect the environment in every way for the benefit of both present and future generations;
		17	create and operate a world economic development organization to serve equitably the needs of all nations and people included within the world federation of nations;

		18	develop and implement solutions to transnational problems of food supply, agricultural production, soil fertility, soil conservation, pest control, diet, nutrition, drugs and poisons, and the disposal of toxic wastes;
		19	develop and implement means to control population growth in relation to the life-support capacities of earth and solve problems of population distribution;
		20	develop, protect, regulate, and conserve the water supplies of earth; develop, operate, and/or coordinate transnational irrigation and other water supply and control projects; assure equitable allocation of transnational water supplies and protect against adverse transnational effects of water or moisture diversion or weather control projects within national boundaries;
		21	own, administer, and supervise the development and conservation of the oceans and seabeds of earth and all resources thereof and protect from damage;
		22	protect from damage and control and supervise the uses of the atmosphere of earth;
		23	conduct interplanetary and cosmic explorations and research; have exclusive jurisdiction over the moon and over all satellites launched from earth;
		24	establish, operate, and/or coordinate global airlines, ocean transport systems, international railways and highways, global communication systems, and means for interplanetary travel and communications; control and administer vital waterways;
		25	develop, operate, and/or coordinate transnational power systems or networks of small units, integrating into the systems or networks power derived from the sun, wind, water, tides, heat differentials, magnetic forces, and any other source of safe, ecologically sound, and continuing energy supply;
		26	control the mining, production, transportation, and use of fossil sources of energy to the extent necessary to reduce and prevent damages to the environment and the ecology, as well as to prevent conflicts and conserve supplies for sustained use by succeeding generations;

		27	exercise exclusive jurisdiction and control over nuclear energy research and testing and nuclear power production, including the right to prohibit any form of testing or production considered hazardous;
		28	place under world controls essential natural resources that may be limited or unevenly distributed about the earth; find and implement ways to reduce wastes and find ways to minimize disparities when development or production is insufficient to supply everybody with all that may be needed;
		29	provide for the examination and assessment of technological innovations that are or may be of supranational consequence, to determine possible hazards or perils to humanity or the environment; institute such controls and regulations of technology as may be found necessary to prevent or correct widespread hazards or perils to human health and welfare;
		30	carry out intensive programs to develop safe alternatives to any technology or technological processes that may be hazardous to the environment, the ecological system, or human health and welfare;
		31	resolve supranational problems caused by gross disparities in technological development or capability, capital formation, availability of natural resources, educational opportunity, economic opportunity, and wage and price differentials; assist the processes of technology transfer under conditions that safeguard human welfare and the environment and contribute to minimizing disparities;
		32	intervene under procedures to be defined by the World Parliament in cases of both intrastate violence and intrastate problems that seriously affect world peace or universal human rights;
		33	develop a world university system; obtain the correction of prejudicial communicative materials that cause misunderstandings or conflicts because of differences of race, religion, sex, national origin, or affiliation;

		34	designate as may be found desirable an official world language or official world languages;
		35	establish and operate a system of world parks, wild life preserves, natural places, and wilderness areas;
		36	define and establish procedures for initiative and referendum by the citizens of earth on matters of supranational legislation not prohibited by this World Constitution;
		37	establish such departments, bureaus, commissions, institutes, corporations, administrations, or agencies as may be needed to carry out any and all the functions and powers of the world government;
		38	serve the needs of humanity in any and all ways that are now or may prove in the future to be beyond the capacity of national and local governments;
		39	to approve the appointments of the heads of all major departments, commissions, offices, agencies, and other parts of the several organs of the world government; and to
		40	remove from office for cause any member of the world executive and any appointed head of any organ, department, office, agency, or other part of the world government, subject to the specific provisions in this World Constitution concerning specific offices.
	Sec. B		**Features of the New World Government** The new world government shall stand out as an effective organisation offering definitive solutions to old and new human problems such as war and the development of weapons of mass destruction, global poverty and inequality, and environmental degradation and work towards nuclear nonproliferation and disarmament. The world government will also satisfy the requirements of freedom—the world will be poised to break free of both capitalism and imperialism; unity—the world can be united, overcoming both the east-west and the north-south divides; world peace—the world can begin disarmament, replacing the war system with a world peace system; human rights—economic and political institutions will be put in place to protect human rights

			worldwide; and sustainability—institutions will be put in place to ensure a sustainable world system. Participation of the people and all nations of the world is ensured in the operation of the world government.
	Sec. C		**Directive Principles for the New World Government** It shall be the aim of the world government to secure certain other rights for all inhabitants within the world government, but without immediate guarantee of universal achievement and enforcement. These rights are defined as directive principles, obligating the world government to pursue every reasonable means for universal realization and implementation and shall include the following:
		1.	equal opportunity for useful employment for everyone, with wages or remuneration sufficient to assure human dignity;
		2.	freedom of choice in work, occupation, employment, or profession;
		3.	full access to information and to the accumulated knowledge of the human race;
		4.	free and adequate public education available to everyone, extending to the pre-university level; equal opportunities for elementary and higher education for all persons; equal opportunity for continued education for all persons throughout life; and the right of any person or parent to choose a private educational institution at any time;
		5.	free and adequate public health services and medical care available to everyone throughout life under conditions of free choice;
		6.	equal opportunity for leisure time for everyone; better distribution of the workload of society so that every person may have equitable leisure time opportunities;
		7.	equal opportunity for everyone to enjoy the benefits of scientific and technological discoveries and developments;
		8.	protection for everyone against the hazards and perils of technological innovations and developments;

		9.	protection of the natural environment, which is the common heritage of humanity against pollution, ecological disruption, or damage, which could imperil life or lower the quality of life;
		10	conservation of those natural resources of earth that are limited so that present and future generations may continue to enjoy life on the planet Earth;
		11	assurance for everyone of adequate housing, of adequate and nutritious food supplies, of safe and adequate water supplies, of pure air with protection of oxygen supplies and the ozone layer, and in general for the continuance of an environment that can sustain healthy living for all; assure to each child the right to the full realization of his or her potential;
		12	assure to each child the right to the full realization of his or her potential;
		13	social security for everyone to relieve the hazards of unemployment, sickness, old age, family circumstances, disability, catastrophes of nature, and technological change, and to allow retirement with sufficient lifetime income for living under conditions of human dignity during older age;
		14	rapid elimination of and prohibitions against technological hazards and man-made environmental disturbances that are found to create dangers to life on earth;
		15	implementation of intensive programs to discover, develop, and institute safe alternatives and practical substitutions for technologies that must be eliminated and prohibited because of hazards and dangers to life;
		16	encouragement for cultural diversity; encouragement for decentralized administration;
		17	freedom for peaceful self-determination for minorities, refugees, and dissenters;
		18	freedom for change of residence to anywhere on earth conditioned by provisions for temporary sanctuaries in events of large numbers of refugees, stateless persons, or mass migrations; and
		19	prohibition against the death penalty.

Article 5			**The World Parliament**
			The World Parliament is formed through proportional representation of nations' parliaments. There are two methods of calculating the proportionality of participation of countries' members of Parliament in the World Parliament. The first method is to calculate the proportionality on the basis of the countries' share of world population as indicated in annexure 2. This method shows wide variations in the countries' contribution of MPs because of their huge population differences.
			The new federal world government covers the seven world continents for its governance. However, only six continents (except Antarctica) are represented in the in the new federal world government formation. The second method is to calculate the proportionality on the basis of the six continents and their countries (annexure 4).
	Sec. A		**Functions and Powers of the World Parliament**
		1.	To prepare and enact detailed legislation in all areas of authority and jurisdiction granted to the world government under article 4 of this World Constitution
		2.	To amend or repeal world laws as may be found necessary or desirable
		3.	To approve, amend, or reject the international laws developed prior to the advent of world government, and to codify and integrate the system of world law and world legislation under the world government
		4.	To establish such regulations and directions as may be needed, consistent with this World Constitution, for the proper functioning of all organs, branches, departments, bureaus, commissions, institutes, agencies, or parts of the world government.

		5.	To review, amend, and give final approval to each budget for the world government, as submitted by the world executive; to devise the specific means for directly raising funds needed to fulfil the budget, including taxes, licenses, fees, globally accounted social and public costs that must be added into the prices for goods and services, loans and credit advances, and any other appropriate means; and to appropriate and allocate funds for all operations and functions of the world government in accordance with approved budgets, but subject to the right of the parliament to revise any appropriation not yet spent or contractually committed
		6.	To create, alter, abolish, or consolidate the departments, bureaus, commissions, institutes, agencies, or other parts of the world government as may be needed for the best functioning of the several organs of the world government, subject to the specific provisions of this World Constitution
	Sec. B		**Composition and Tenure of the World Parliament**
		1.	The World Parliament is formed through proportional representation of nation's parliaments and consists of the following two houses: (a) upper house (b) lower house
		2.	**Proportional Representation** (a) The World Parliament will have 'treasury benches.' The treasury benches will be composed of the members of Parliament of nations' parliament proportional to their share of the world population with at least a minimum of one member of Parliament represented. (b) The World Parliament will have 'opposition benches' as well to play a 'watchdog' role with proportional representation of nations' opposition parties limited to 10 per cent of the treasury bench proportionate with at least a minimum of one member of Parliament represented.
		3.	All members of the World Parliament, regardless of house, shall be designated as members of the World Parliament.

		4.	This will form the legislative wing of the world government.
		5.	Thus, the World Parliament will not get involved in any 'election process' on its own.
		6.	The tenure of the World Parliament will be five years at a time.
	Sec. C		**The Upper House** The upper house is presided over by the chairman assisted by five deputy chairmen representing the remaining five continental areas and to be elected by the house.
	Sec. D		**The Lower House** The lower house is presided over by the speaker assisted by five deputy speakers representing the other five continental areas. They will be elected by the lower house.
	Sec. E		**Procedures of the World Parliament**
		1.	Each house of the World Parliament during its first session shall elect a panel of six chairpersons from amongst its own members, one from each of six continental divisions. The chairpersons shall rotate annually so that each will serve for one year as chief presiding officer, while the other five serve as vice chairpersons.
		2.	The panels of chairpersons from each house shall meet together, as needed, for the purpose of coordinating the work of the houses of the World Parliament, both severally and jointly.
		3.	Any legislative measure or action may be initiated in either house or both concurrently and shall become effective when passed by a simple majority vote of both the houses except in those cases where an absolute majority vote or other voting majority is specified in this World Constitution.
		4.	Each house of the World Parliament shall adopt its own detailed rules of procedure, which shall be consistent with the procedures set forth in this World Constitution, and which shall be designed to facilitate coordinated functioning of the two houses.

		5.	Approval of appointments by the World Parliament shall require simple majority votes, while removals for cause shall require absolute majority votes.
		6.	The World Parliament shall remain in session for a minimum of nine months of each year. One or two breaks may be taken during each year, at times and for durations to be decided by simple majority vote of both the houses sitting jointly.
		7.	Annual salaries for members of the World Parliament of all two houses shall be the same, except for those who serve also as members of the presidium and of the executive cabinet.
		8.	Salary schedules for members of the World Parliament and for members of the presidium and of the executive cabinet shall be determined by the World Parliament.
Article 6			**The World Executive**
	Sec. A		**World Executive** The world executive shall be constituted by the World Parliament. The world executive shall consist of a presidium of six members and of an executive cabinet of sixty members all of whom shall be members of the World Parliament.
	Sec. B		**Functions and Powers of the World Executive**
		1.	To implement the basic system of world law as defined in the World Constitution and in the codified system of world law after approval by the World Parliament To implement legislation enacted by the World Parliament
		2.	To implement legislation enacted by the World Parliament
		3.	To propose and recommend legislation for enactment by the World Parliament
		4.	To convene the World Parliament in special sessions when necessary
		5.	To supervise the world administration and the integrative complex and all of the departments, bureaus, offices, institutes, and agencies thereof

		6.	To nominate, select, and remove the heads of various organs, branches, departments, bureaus, offices, commissions, institutes, agencies, and other parts of the world government in accordance with the provisions of this World Constitution and as specified in measures enacted by the World Parliament
		7.	To prepare and submit annually to the World Parliament a comprehensive budget for the operations of the world government and to prepare and submit periodically budget projections over periods of several years
		8.	To define and propose priorities for world legislation and budgetary allocations
		9.	To be held accountable to the World Parliament for the expenditures of appropriations made by the World Parliament in accordance with approved and longer term budgets, subject to revisions approved by the World Parliament.
	Sec. C		**The Presidium**
		1.	The presidium shall be composed of six members, one to be designated as president and the other five to be designated as vice presidents. Each member of the presidium shall be from a different continental division.
		2.	Each member of the presidium shall be a member of the World Parliament.
		3.	Nominations for the presidium shall be made by the treasury bench of the lower house of the World Parliament. Similarly, the leader of opposition will be nominated by the opposition bench in both the houses of the World Parliament.
		4.	Members of the presidium may be removed for cause, either individually or collectively, by an absolute majority vote of the combined membership of the two houses of the World Parliament in joint session.

		5.	The term of office for the presidium shall be five years and shall run concurrently with the terms of office for the members as members of the World Parliament, except that at the end of each five-year period, the presidium members in office shall continue to serve until the new presidium for the succeeding term is formed. Membership in the presidium shall be limited to two consecutive terms.
	Sec. D		**The Executive Cabinet**
		1.	The executive cabinet shall be composed of sixty members.
		2.	All members of the executive cabinet shall be members of the World Parliament.
		3.	There shall be no more than two members of the executive cabinet from any single nation of the world government. There may be only one member of the executive cabinet from a nation from which a member of the World Parliament is serving as a member of the presidium.
		4.	Each member of the executive cabinet shall serve as the head of a department or agency of the world administration and in this capacity shall be designated as minister of the particular department or agency.
		5.	Nominations for members of the executive cabinet shall be made by the presidium, taking into consideration the various functions that executive cabinet members are to perform.
		6.	The executive cabinet shall be elected by simple majority vote of the combined membership of all two houses of the World Parliament in joint session.
		7.	Members of the executive cabinet, either individually or collectively, may be removed for cause by an absolute majority vote of the combined membership of all two houses of the World Parliament sitting in joint session.

		8.	The term of office in the executive cabinet shall be five years and shall run concurrently with the terms of office for the members as members of the World Parliament, except that at the end of each five-year period, the cabinet members in office shall continue to serve until the new executive cabinet for the succeeding term is formed. Membership in the executive cabinet shall be limited to three consecutive terms, regardless of change in ministerial position.
	Sec. E		**Procedures of the World Executive**
		1.	The presidium shall assign the ministerial positions amongst the cabinet members to head the several administrative departments and major agencies of the administration and of the integrative complex. Each vice president may also serve as a minister to head an administrative department, but not the president. Ministerial positions may be changed at the discretion of the presidium. A cabinet member or vice president may hold more than one ministerial post, but no more than three, provided that no cabinet member is without a ministerial post.
		2.	The presidium, in consultation with the executive cabinet, shall prepare and present to the World Parliament near the beginning of each year a proposed program of world legislation. The presidium may propose other legislations during the year.
		3.	The presidium, in consultation with the executive cabinet, and in consultation with the world financial administration, shall be responsible for preparing and submitting to the World Parliament the proposed annual budget and budgetary projections over periods of years.
		4.	Each cabinet member and vice president as minister of a particular department or agency shall prepare an annual report for the particular department or agency, to be submitted both to the presidium and to the World Parliament.
		5.	The members of the presidium and of the executive cabinet at all times shall be responsible both individually and collectively to the World Parliament.

		6.	Vacancies occurring at any time in the world executive shall be filled within sixty days by nomination and election in the same manner as specified for filling the offices originally
	Sec. F		**Limitations of the World Executive**
		1.	The world executive shall not at any time alter, suspend, abridge, infringe, or otherwise violate any provision of this World Constitution or any legislation or world law enacted or approved by the World Parliament in accordance with the provisions of this World Constitution.
		2.	The world executive shall not have veto power over any legislation passed by the World Parliament.
		3.	The world executive may not dissolve the World Parliament or any house of the World Parliament.
		4.	The world executive may not act contrary to decisions of the world courts.
		5.	The world executive shall be bound to faithfully execute all legislation passed by the World Parliament in accordance with the provisions of this World Constitution, and may not impound or refuse to spend funds appropriated by the World Parliament, or spend more funds than are appropriated by the World Parliament.
		6.	The world executive may not transcend or contradict the decisions or controls of the World Parliament, the world judiciary, or the provisions of this World Constitution by any device of executive order or executive privilege or emergency declaration or decree
Article 7			**The World Administration**
	Sec. A		**Functions of the World Administration**
		1.	The world administration shall be organized to carry out the detailed and continuous administration and implementation of world legislation and world law.
		2.	The world administration shall be under the direction of the world executive and shall at all times be responsible to the world executive.

		3.	The world administration shall be organized so as to give professional continuity to the work of administration and implementation.
	Sec. B		**Structure and Procedures of the World Administration**
		1.	The world administration shall be composed of professionally organized departments and other agencies in all areas of activity requiring continuity of administration and implementation by the world government.
		2.	Each department or major agency of the world administration shall be headed by a minister, who shall be either a member of the executive cabinet or a vice president of the presidium.
		3.	Each department or major agency of the world administration shall have as principal secretary a senior administrator, who shall assist the minister and supervise the detailed work of the department or agency.
		4.	Each senior administrator shall be nominated by the minister of the particular department or agency from amongst persons in the senior lists of the world civil service administration, as soon as senior lists have been established by the world civil service administration, and shall be confirmed by the presidium. Temporary qualified appointments shall be made by the ministers, with confirmation by the presidium, pending establishment of the senior lists.
		5.	There shall be a cabinet secretary of the world administration, who shall be nominated by the presidium and confirmed by absolute majority vote of the entire executive cabinet.
		6.	The functions and responsibilities of the cabinet secretary of the world administration shall be to assist in coordinating the work of the senior administrators of the several departments and agencies of the world administration. The cabinet secretary shall at all times be subject to the direction of the presidium and shall be directly responsible to the presidium.

			7.	The employment of any senior administrator and of the cabinet secretary may be terminated for cause by absolute majority vote of both the executive cabinet and presidium combined, but not contrary to civil service rules that protect tenure on grounds of competence.
			8.	Each minister of a department or agency of the world administration, being also a member of the World Parliament, shall provide continuous liaison between the particular department or agency and the World Parliament, shall respond at any time to any questions or requests for information from the parliament, including committees of any house of the World Parliament.
			9.	The presidium, in cooperation with the particular ministers in each case, shall be responsible for the original organization of each of the departments and major agencies of the world administration.
			10	The assignment of legislative measures, constitutional provisions, and areas of world law to particular departments and agencies for administration and implementation shall be done by the presidium in consultation with the executive cabinet and cabinet secretary, unless specifically provided in legislation passed by the World Parliament.
			11	The presidium, in consultation with the executive cabinet, may propose the creation of other departments and agencies to have ministerial status and may propose the alteration, combination, or termination of existing departments and agencies of ministerial status as may seem necessary or desirable. Any such creation, alteration, combination, or termination shall require a simple majority vote of approval of the two houses of the World Parliament in joint session.
			12	The World Parliament by absolute majority vote of the two houses in joint session may specify the creation of new departments or agencies of ministerial status in the world administration or may direct the world executive to alter, combine, or terminate existing departments or agencies of ministerial status.

		13	The presidium and the world executive may not create, establish, or maintain any administrative or executive department or agency for the purpose of circumventing control by the World Parliament.
	Sec. C		**Departments of the World Administration** Amongst the departments and agencies of the world administration of ministerial status, but not limited thereto and subject to combinations and to changes in descriptive terminology, shall be those listed under this section. Each major area of administration shall be headed by a cabinet minister and a senior administrator, or by a vice president and a senior administrator. 1. disarmament and war prevention 2. population 3. food and agriculture 4. water supplies and waterways 5. health and nutrition 6. education 7. cultural diversity and the arts 8. habitat and settlements 9. environment and ecology 10. world resources 11. oceans and seabeds 12. atmosphere and space 13. energy 14. science and technology 15. genetic research and engineering 16. labour and income 17. economic and social development 18. commerce and industry 19. transportation and travel 20. multinational corporations 21. communications and information 22. human rights 23. distributive justice

			24. world service corps
			25. world territories, capitals, and parks
			26. exterior relations
			27. democratic procedures
			28. revenue
			29. defence
			30. home affairs
Article 8			**The Supportive Divisions**
	Sec. A		**Definition**
		1.	Certain administrative, research, planning, and facilitative agencies of the world government, which are particularly essential for the satisfactory functioning of all or most aspects of the world government, shall be designated as the supportive wings. The supportive wings shall include the agencies listed under this section, with the proviso that other such agencies may be added upon recommendation of the presidium followed by decision of the World Parliament. a) the Division of World Civil Services b) the Division of Governmental Procedures and World Problems c) the Division of Research and Planning d) the Division of Technological and Environmental Assessment e) the Division of World Financial Administration f) the Commission for Legislative Review
		2.	Each agency of the supportive divisions shall be headed by a cabinet minister and a senior administrator, or by a vice president and a senior administrator, together with a commission as provided hereunder. The rules of procedure for each agency shall be decided by majority decision of the commission members together with the administrator and the minister or vice president.

		3.	The World Parliament may at any time define further the responsibilities, functioning, and organization of the several agencies of the supportive division, consistent with the provisions of the World Constitution.
		4.	Each agency of the supportive division shall make an annual report to the World Parliament and to the presidium.
	Sec. B		**The Division of World Civil Service**
		1.	The functions of the Division of World Civil Service shall be the following, but not limited thereto:
			a) To formulate and define standards, qualifications, tests, examinations, and salary scales for the personnel of all organs, departments, bureaus, offices, commissions, and agencies of the world government, in conformity with the provisions of this World Constitution and requiring approval by the presidium and executive cabinet, subject to review and approval by the World Parliament.
			b) To establish rosters or lists of competent personnel for all categories of personnel to be appointed or employed in the service of the world government.
			c) To select and employ upon request by any government organ, department, bureau, office, institute, commission, agency, or authorized official such competent personnel as may be needed and authorized, except for those positions that are made elective or appointive under provisions of the World Constitution or by specific legislation of the World Parliament.
		2.	The Division of World Civil Services shall be headed by a ten-member commission in addition to the cabinet minister or vice president and senior administrator.

	Sec. C		**The Division of Governmental Procedures and World Problems**
		1.	The functions of the Division of Governmental Procedures and World Problems shall be as follows but not limited thereto
			a) to prepare and conduct courses of information, education, and training for all personnel in the service of the world government, including members of the World Parliament and of all other elective, appointive, and civil service personnel, so that every person in the service of the world government may have a better understanding of the functions, structure, procedures, and interrelationships of the various organs, departments, bureaus, offices, institutes, commissions, agencies, and other parts of the world government;
			b) to prepare and conduct courses and seminars for information, education, discussion, updating, and new ideas in all areas of world problems, particularly for members of the World Parliament and of the world executive, and for the chief personnel of all organs, departments, and agencies of the world government, but open to all in the service of the world government;
			c) to bring in qualified persons from private and public universities, colleges, and research and action organizations of many countries, as well as other qualified persons, to lecture and to be resource persons for the courses and seminars organized by the Governmental Procedures and World Problems Wing; and
			d) to contract with private or public universities and colleges or other agencies to conduct courses and seminars for the institute.

		2.	The Division of Governmental Procedures and World Problems shall be supervised by a ten-member commission in addition to the senior administrator and cabinet minister or vice president. The commission shall be composed of two commissioners each to be named by both the houses of parliament, the presidium, the Collegium of World Judges, the World Attorneys General Office, the Division of Research and Planning, the Division of Technological and Environmental Assessment, and the Division of World Financial Administration. Commissioners shall serve five-year terms and may serve consecutive terms.
	Sec. D		**The Division of Research and Planning**
		1.	The functions of the Division of Research and Planning shall be as follows but not limited thereto
			a) to serve the World Parliament, the world executive, the world administration, and other organs, departments, and agencies of the world government in any matter requiring research and planning within the competence of the agency;
			b) to prepare and maintain a comprehensive inventory of world resources;
			c) to prepare comprehensive long-range plans for the development, conservation, recycling, and equitable sharing of the resources of earth for the benefit of all people on earth, subject to legislative action by the World Parliament;
			d) to prepare and maintain a comprehensive list and description of all world problems, including their interrelationships, impact time projections, and proposed solutions, together with bibliographies;
			e) to do research and help prepare legislative measures at the request of any member of the World Parliament or of any committee of any house of the World Parliament;

			f)	to do research and help prepare proposed legislation or proposed legislative programs and schedules at the request of the presidium or executive cabinet or of any cabinet minister;
			g)	to do research and prepare reports at the request of any other organ, department, or agency of the world government;
			h)	to enlist the help of public and private universities, colleges, research agencies, and other associations and organizations for various research and planning projects;
			i)	to contract with public and private universities, colleges, research agencies, and other organizations for the preparation of specific reports, studies, and proposals; and
			j)	to maintain a comprehensive world library for the use of all members of the World Parliament, and for the use of all other officials and persons in the service of the world government, as well as for public information.
		2.		The Division of Research and Planning shall be supervised by a ten-member commission in addition to the senior administrator and cabinet minister or vice president. The commission shall be composed of two commissioners each to be named by both the houses of parliament, the presidium, the Collegium of World Judges, the World Attorneys General Office, the Division of Research and Planning, the Division of Technological and Environmental Assessment, and the Division of World Financial Administration. Commissioners shall serve five-year terms and may serve consecutive terms.
	Sec. E			**The Division of Technological and Environmental Assessment**
		1.		The functions of the Division of Technological and Environmental Assessment shall include the following, but not limited thereto:

a) To establish and maintain a registration and description of all significant technological innovations, together with impact projections.

b) To examine, analyse, and assess the impacts and consequences of technological innovations that may have either significant beneficial or significant harmful or dangerous consequences for human life or for the ecology of life on earth, or that may require particular regulations or prohibitions to prevent or eliminate dangers or to assure benefits.

c) To examine, analyse, and assess environmental and ecological problems, in particular the environmental and ecological problems that may result from any intrusions or changes of the environment or ecological relationships, which may be caused by technological innovations, processes of resource development, patterns of human settlements, the production of energy, patterns of economic and industrial development, or other man-made intrusions and changes of the environment, or which may result from natural causes.

d) To maintain a global monitoring network to measure possible harmful effects of technological innovations and environmental disturbances so that corrective measures can be designed.

e) To prepare recommendations based on technological and environmental analyses and assessments, which can serve as guides to the World Parliament, the world executive, the world administration, the Division of Research and Planning, and to the other organs, departments, and divisions of the world government, as well as to individuals in the service of the world government and to national and local governments and legislative bodies.

			f) To enlist the voluntary or contractual aid and participation of private and public universities, colleges, research institutions, and other associations and organizations in the work of technological and environmental assessment.
			g) To enlist the voluntary or contractual aid and participation of private and public universities and colleges, research institutions, and other organizations in devising and developing alternatives to harmful or dangerous technologies and environmentally disruptive activities, and in devising controls to assure beneficial results from technological innovations or to prevent harmful results from either technological innovations or environmental changes, all subject to legislation for implementation by the World Parliament.
		2.	The Division of Technological and Environmental Assessment shall be supervised by a six-member commission in addition to the senior administrator and cabinet minister or vice president. The persons to serve as commissioners shall be nominated by both the houses of parliament and then appointed by the world presidium for five-year terms. Commissioners may serve consecutive terms.
	Sec. F		**The Division of World Financial Administration**
		1.	The functions of the Division of World Financial Administration shall include the following, but not limited thereto:
			a) To establish and operate the procedures for the collection of revenues for the world government, pursuant to legislation by the World Parliament, inclusive of taxes, globally accounted social and public costs, licenses, fees, revenue sharing arrangements, income derived from supranational public enterprises or projects or resource developments, and all other sources.

b) To operate a planetary accounting office and thereunder to make cost/benefit studies and reports of the functioning and activities of the world government and of its several organs, departments, branches, bureaus, offices, commissions, institutes, agencies, and other parts or projects; in making such studies and reports, account shall be taken not only of direct financial costs and benefits but also of human, social, environmental, indirect, long-term, and other costs and benefits, and of actual or possible hazards and damages. Such studies and reports shall also be designed to uncover any wastes, inefficiencies, misapplications, corruptions, diversions, unnecessary costs, and other possible irregularities.

c) To make cost/benefit studies and reports at the request of any house or committee of the World Parliament, and of the presidium, the executive cabinet, the Office of World Attorneys General, the World Supreme Court, or of any administrative department or any agency of the integrative complex, as well as upon its own initiative.

d) To operate a Planetary Comptroller's Office and thereunder to supervise the disbursement of the funds of the world government for all purposes, projects, and activities duly authorized by this World Constitution, the World Parliament, the world executive, and other organs, departments, and divisions of the world government.

e) To establish and operate a planetary banking system, making the transition to a common global currency, under the terms of specific legislation passed by the World Parliament.

f) Pursuant to specific legislation enacted by the World Parliament, and in conjunction with the planetary banking system, to establish and implement the procedures of a planetary monetary and credit system based upon useful productive capacity and performance, both in goods and services. Such a monetary and credit system shall be designed for use within the planetary banking system for the financing of the activities and projects of the world government, and for all other financial purposes approved by the World Parliament, without requiring the payment of interest on bonds, investments, or other claims of financial ownership or debt.

g) To establish criteria for the extension of financial credit based upon such considerations as people available to work, usefulness, cost/benefit accounting, human and social values, environmental health and aesthetics, minimizing disparities, integrity, competent management, appropriate technology, potential production and performance.

h) To establish and operate a planetary insurance system in areas of world need that transcend national boundaries and in accordance with legislation passed by the World Parliament.

i) To assist the presidium as may be requested in the technical preparation of budgets for the operation of the world government.

2. The Division of World Financial Administration shall be supervised by a commission of eight members, together with a senior administrator and a cabinet minister or vice president. The commission shall be composed of one commissioner each to be named by the both the houses of parliament, the presidium, the Collegium of World Judges, the Office of Attorneys General, the Division of Research and Planning, the Division of Technological and Environmental Assessment, and the Institute on Governmental Procedures and World Problems. Commissioners shall serve terms of five years and may serve consecutive terms.

	Sec. G		**Commission for Legislative Review**
		1.	The functions of the Commission for Legislative Review shall be to examine world legislation and world laws that the World Parliament enacts or adopts from the previous body of international law for the purpose of analysing whether any particular legislation or law has become obsolete or obstructive or defective in serving the purposes intended; and to make recommendations to the World Parliament accordingly for repeal or amendment or replacement.
		2.	The Commission for Legislative Review shall be composed of six members, including two each to be elected by the both the houses of parliament, the Collegium of World Judges, and the presidium. Members of the commission shall serve terms of ten years and may be re-elected to serve consecutive terms. One half of the commission members after the commission is first formed shall be elected every five years, with the first terms for one half of the members to be only five years.
Article 9			**The World Judiciary**
	Sec. A		**Jurisdiction of the World Supreme Court**
		1.	A World Supreme Court shall be established, together with such regional world courts as may subsequently be found necessary. The World Supreme Court shall comprise a number of benches.
		2.	The World Supreme Court, together with such regional world courts as may be established, shall have mandatory jurisdiction in all cases, actions, disputes, conflicts, violations of law, civil suits, guarantees of civil and human rights, constitutional interpretations, and other litigations arising under the provisions of this World Constitution, world legislation, and the body of world law approved by the World Parliament.
		3.	Decisions of the World Supreme Court shall be binding on all parties involved in all cases, actions, and litigations brought before any bench of the World Supreme Court for settlement. Each bench of the World Supreme Court shall constitute a court of highest appeal.

	Sec. B		**Benches of the World Supreme Court**
			The benches of the World Supreme Court and their respective jurisdictions shall be as follows:
		1.	**Bench for Human Rights:** To deal with issues of human rights arising under the guarantee of civil and human rights provided by Article XIV of this World Constitution, and arising in pursuance of the provisions of Article XIV of this World Constitution, and arising otherwise under world legislation and the body of world law approved by the World Parliament.
		2.	**Bench for Criminal Cases:** To deal with issues arising from the violation of world laws and world legislation by individuals, corporations, groups, and associations, but not issues primarily concerned with human rights.
		3.	**Bench for Civil Cases:** To deal with issues involving civil law suits and disputes between individuals, corporations, groups, and associations arising under world legislation and world law and the administration thereof.
		4.	**Bench for Constitutional Cases:** To deal with the interpretation of the World Constitution and with issues and actions arising in connection with the interpretation of the World Constitution.
		5.	**Bench for International Conflicts:** To deal with disputes, conflicts, and legal contest arising between or amongst the nations that have joined in the new world government.
		6.	**Bench for Public Cases:** To deal with issues not under the jurisdiction of another bench arising from conflicts, disputes, civil suits, or other legal contests between the world government and corporations, groups, or individuals, or between national governments and corporations, groups, or individuals in cases involving world legislation and world law.
		7.	**Appellate Bench:** To deal with issues involving world legislation and world law that may be appealed from national courts; and to decide which bench to assign a case or action or litigation when a question or disagreement arises over the proper jurisdiction.

		8.	**Advisory Bench:** To give opinions upon request on any legal question arising under world law or world legislation, exclusive of contests or actions involving interpretation of the World Constitution. Advisory opinions may be requested by any house or committee of the World Parliament, by the presidium, any administrative department, the Office of World Attorneys General, or by any agency of the integrative complex.
		9.	**Other benches** may be established, combined, or terminated upon recommendation of the Collegium of World Judges with approval by the World Parliament; but benches number one through eight may not be combined or terminated except by amendment of this World Constitution.
	Sec. C		**Seats of the World Supreme Court**
		1.	The primary seat of the World Supreme Court and all benches shall be the same as for the location of the primary world capital and for the location of the World Parliament and the World Executive.
		2.	Continental seats of the World Supreme Court shall be established in the five secondary capitals of the world government located in five different continental divisions of earth.
		3.	The following permanent benches of the World Supreme Court shall be established both at the primary seat and at each of the continental seats: human rights, criminal cases, civil cases, and public cases.
		4.	The following permanent benches of the World Supreme Court shall be located only at the primary seat of the World Supreme Court: constitutional cases, international conflicts, appellate bench, and advisory bench.
		5.	Benches that are located permanently only at the primary seat of the World Supreme Court may hold special sessions at the other continental seats of the World Supreme Court when necessary or may establish continental circuits if needed.

		6.	Benches of the World Supreme Court that have permanent continental locations may hold special sessions at other locations when needed, or may establish regional circuits if needed.
	Sec. D		**The Collegium of World Judges**
		1.	A Collegium of World Judges shall be established by the World Parliament. The collegium shall consist of a minimum of twenty-member judges and may be expanded as needed but not to exceed sixty members.
		2.	The world judges to compose the Collegium of World Judges shall be nominated by the parliament.
		3.	The term of office for a world judge shall be ten years. Successive terms may be served without limit.
		4.	The Collegium of World Judges shall elect a Presiding Council of World Judges, consisting of a chief justice and five associate chief justices. One member of the Presiding Council of World Judges shall be elected from each of six continental divisions of the globe. Members of the Presiding Council of World Judges shall serve five-year terms on the presiding council and may serve two successive terms, but not two successive terms as chief justice.
		5.	The Presiding Council of World Judges shall assign all world judges, including themselves, to the several benches of the World Supreme Court. Each bench for a sitting at each location shall have a minimum of three world judges, except that the number of world judges for benches on continental cases and international conflicts, and the appellate bench, shall be no less than five.
		6.	The member judges of each bench at each location shall choose annually a presiding judge, who may serve two successive terms.
		7.	The members of the several benches may be reconstituted from time to time as may seem desirable or necessary upon the decision of the Presiding Council of World Judges. Any decision to reconstitute a bench shall be referred to a vote of the entire Collegium of World Judges by request of any world judge.

		8.	Any world judge may be removed from office for cause by an absolute two-thirds majority vote of the two houses of the World Parliament in joint session.
		9.	Qualifications for judges of the World Supreme Court shall be at least ten years of legal or juristic experience, minimum age of thirty years, and evident competence in world law and the humanities.
		10	The salaries, expenses, remunerations, and prerogatives of the world judges shall be determined by the World Parliament and shall be reviewed every five years, but shall not be changed to the disadvantage of any world judge during a term of office. All members of the Collegium of World Judges shall receive the same salaries, except that additional compensation may be given to the Presiding Council of World Judges.
		11	Upon recommendation by the Collegium of World Judges, the World Parliament shall have the authority to establish regional and district world courts below the World Supreme Court, and to establish the jurisdictions thereof, and the procedures for appeal to the World Supreme Court or to the several benches thereof.
		12	The detailed rules of procedure for the functioning of the World Supreme Court, the Collegium of World Judges, and for each bench of the World Supreme Court shall be decided and amended by absolute majority vote of the Collegium of World Judges.
Article 10			**World Army**
		1.	Each member country will prune its army strength at least by 50 per cent and will contribute the same on deputation to the World Army (includes army, navy, and air force).
		2.	The contributions of army from all the member countries will thus form the World Army.
		3.	The chiefs of army will be appointed by the world cabinet.
Article 11			**World Intelligence Agency**
		1.	The world government will constitute its own Intelligence Agency (WIA).

		2.	The service conditions and functions will be of world standards.
Article 12			**World Police System**
		1.	The world government will constitute the World Police System to maintain law and order.
		2.	The service conditions and functions will be on par with world standards.
Article 13	Sec. A		**World Cultural Council and World Cultural Centre** The World Cultural Centre will provide full-fledged infrastructure for study, research, and cultural activities, and it will act as a 'melting pot' of east-west-south-north ancient knowledge, wisdom, languages, and cultures for the well-being of humanity. It will be governed by a World Cultural Council (WCC). The council will be represented on a linguistic basis, with each language of the world represented, and will be made up of intellectuals, writers, poets, philologists, and philosophers. About four billion of the earth's 6.5 billion people, or over 60 per cent of the earth's population, speak one of the main thirty languages as their native tongue: Chinese (Mandarin), Hindi, Spanish, English, Arabic, Portuguese, Bengali, Russian, Japanese, German, Panjabi, Javanese, Korean, Vietnamese, Telugu, Marathi, Tamil, French, Urdu, Italian, Turkish, Persian, Gujarati, Polish, Ukrainian, Malayalam, Kannada, Oriya, Burmese, and Thai. Adding another of the two hundred most populous languages on the planet and we would have about four hundred delegates representing these languages. Discussions, debates, round tables, seminars, conferences, and exhibitions on various cultures, traditions, and religious and communal unity and harmony will be held periodically. This may act as a 'think tank' on world cultures, traditions, languages, communal harmony, and human values and offer policy inputs to the world government. The World Cultural Council will be constituted by the World Cabinet for a five-year term and approves adequate budget for the council and the World Cultural Centre.

	Sec. B		**World Interfaith Council**
			Faith is the orderly fashion of any form of belief endowed with exclusive philosophy, customs, and practices. In wider sense, it accommodates all atheistic, sociocentric, and cosmocentric schools like naturalism, socialism, and scientific materialism. In brief, it is the common minimal agenda of all faiths, accepting the need and their role in building a strong, serene, and peaceful earth. The world government supports the World Interfaith Council, which inspires, educates, and mobilizes people to unite across differences and to act from their shared ethical and spiritual values in pursuit of peace. The interfaith council envisions a world free from violence, including the violence of war, poverty, oppression, and environmental devastation. To enact this vision, it commits to nurture a community in which compassion and respect foster actions that dismantle systems of violence while simultaneously creating systems of peace, justice, and ecological sustainability. The interfaith council comprises of leaders of all faiths of the world and social animators. The cabinet will constitute the interfaith council with a five-year term. Adequate budget provision will be made by the world government.
Article 14			**Interface** There shall be an interface mechanism formed between the government, the world governance constituents, civil societies, and the fourth estate to act as a 'global think tank' to advice the world government.
Article 15			**Safeguards and Reservations**
	Sec. A		**Certain Safeguards**
			The world government shall operate to secure for all nations and peoples within the world government the safeguards that are defined hereunder:

		1.	guarantee that full faith and credit shall be given to the public acts, records, legislation, and judicial proceedings of the member nations within the world government, consistent with the several provisions of this World Constitution;
		2.	assure freedom of choice within the member nations and countries of the world government to determine their internal political, economic, and social systems, consistent with the guarantees and protections given under this World Constitution to assure civil liberties and human rights and a safe environment for life, and otherwise consistent with the several provisions of this World Constitution;
		3.	grant the right of asylum within the world government for persons who may seek refuge from countries or nations that are not yet included within the world government;
		4.	grant the right of individuals and groups, after the world government includes 90 per cent of the territory of earth, to peacefully leave the hegemony of the world government and to live in suitable territory set aside by the government neither restricted nor protected by the world government, provided that such territory does not extend beyond 5 per cent of earth's habitable territory, is kept completely disarmed and not used as a base for inciting violence or insurrection within or against the world government or any member nation, and is kept free of acts of environmental or technological damage that seriously affect earth outside such territory.
	Sec. B		**Reservation of Powers** The powers not delegated to the world government by this World Constitution shall be reserved to the nations of the world government and to the people of earth.
Article 16			**Ratification and Implementation**
	Sec. A		**Ratification of the World Constitution** This World Constitution shall be submitted to the nations for ratification by the following procedures:

		1	The World Constitution shall be transmitted to the General Assembly of the United Nations Organization and to each national government on earth, with the request that the World Constitution be submitted to the national legislature of each nation for ratification.
		2	Preliminary ratification by a national legislature shall be accomplished by simple majority vote of the national legislature.
		3	In the case of a nation without a national legislature, the head of the national government shall be requested to give preliminary ratification and to submit the World Constitution for final ratification by popular referendum.
		4	In the case of those nations currently involved in serious international disputes or where traditional enmities and chronic disputes may exist amongst two or more nations, a procedure for concurrent paired ratification shall be instituted whereby the nations that are parties to a current or chronic international dispute or conflict may simultaneously ratify the World Constitution. In such cases, the paired nations shall be admitted into the world government simultaneously, with the obligation for each such nation to immediately turn over all weapons of mass destruction to the world government, and to turn over the conflict or dispute for mandatory peaceful settlement by the world government.
		5	Each nation or political unit that ratifies this World Constitution shall be bound never to use any armed forces or weapons of mass destruction against another member or unit of the world government, regardless of how long it may take to achieve full disarmament of all the nations and political units that ratify this World Constitution.

		6	When ratified, the constitution for the world government becomes the supreme law of earth. By the act of ratifying this World Constitution, any provision in the constitution or legislation of any country so ratifying that is contrary to this World Constitution is either repealed or amended to conform with the constitution for the world government, effective as soon as fifty countries have so ratified. The amendment of national or state constitutions to allow entry into world government is not necessary prior to ratification of the constitution for the world government.
	Sec. B		**Operative Stage of World Government**
		1.	The first operative stage of world government under this World Constitution shall be implemented when the World Constitution is ratified by at least fifty nations.
		2	The nomination of members to the World Parliament by the member nations is completed.
		3	The world presidium and the executive cabinet shall be elected according to the provisions of the constitution by both houses of parliament.
		4	When composed, the presidium for the first operative stage of world government shall assign or reassign ministerial posts amongst cabinet and presidium members and shall immediately establish or confirm a World Disarmament Agency and a World Economic and Development Organization.
		5	Those nations that ratify this World Constitution and thereby join the world government shall immediately transfer all weapons of mass destruction as defined and designated by the World Disarmament Agency to that agency.
		6	The World Disarmament Agency shall immediately immobilize all such weapons and shall proceed with dispatch to dismantle, convert to peacetime use, recycle the materials thereof, or otherwise destroy all such weapons. During the first operative stage of world government, the ratifying nations may retain armed forces equipped with weapons other than weapons of mass destruction as defined and designated by the World Disarmament Agency.

		7	Concurrently with the reduction or elimination of such weapons of mass destruction and other military expenditures as can be accomplished during the first operative stage of world government, the member nations of the world government shall pay annually to the Treasury of the world government amounts equal to one-half the amounts saved from their respective national
		8	military budgets during the last year before joining the world government, and shall continue such payments until the full operative stage of world government is reached. The world government shall use 50 per cent of the funds thus received to finance the work and projects of the World Economic Development Organization.
		9	At the beginning of the first operative stage, the presidium, in consultation with the executive cabinet, shall formulate and put forward a proposed program for solving the most urgent world problems currently confronting humanity.
		10	The World Parliament shall proceed to work upon solutions to world problems. The World Parliament and the World Executive working together shall institute through the several organs, departments, and agencies of the world government whatever means shall seem appropriate and feasible to accomplish the implementation and enforcement of world legislation, world law, and the World Constitution; and in particular shall take certain decisive actions for the welfare of all people on earth, applicable throughout the world, including but not limited to the following:

a) expedite the organization and work of an Emergency Earth Rescue Administration, concerned with all aspects of climate change and climate crises;

b) expedite the new finance, credit, and monetary system to serve human needs;

c) expedite an integrated global energy system, utilizing solar energy, hydrogen energy, and other safe and sustainable sources of energy;

			d) push forward a global program for agricultural production to achieve maximum sustained yield under conditions that are ecologically sound;
			e) establish conditions for free trade within the nations of the world government;
			f) call for and find ways to implement a moratorium on nuclear energy projects until all problems are solved concerning safety, disposal of toxic wastes, and the dangers of use or diversion of materials for the production of nuclear weapons;
			g) outlaw and find ways to completely terminate the production of nuclear weapons and all weapons of mass destruction;
			h) push forward programs to assure adequate and nonpolluted water supplies and clean air supplies for everybody on earth;
			i) push forward a global program to conserve and recycle the resources of earth;
			j) develop an acceptable program to bring population growth under control, especially by raising standards of living.
Article 17			**Amendments**
		1.	Following completion of the operative stage of world government, amendments to this World Constitution may be proposed for consideration by a simple majority vote of any house of the World Parliament.
		2.	Passage of any amendment proposed by a house of the World Parliament shall require an absolute two-thirds majority vote of each of the two houses of the World Parliament voting separately.
		3.	Periodically, but no later than ten years after first convening the World Parliament for the first operative stage of world government, and every twenty years thereafter, the members of the World Parliament shall meet in special session comprising a constitutional convention to conduct a review of this New World Constitution to consider and propose possible amendments, which shall then require action.

		4.	Except by following the amendment procedures specified herein, no part of this New World Constitution may be set aside, suspended, or subverted, neither for emergencies nor caprice nor convenience.

REFERENCES

1. Professor D. Swaminadhan, a concept paper on 'Formation of New World Government—an Innovative Approach' (an Alternative to United Nations Organisation (UNO)).
   https://drive.google.com/file/d/0B6XQmtWYDSfOYVN5ajNlbzRzclU/view?usp=sharing
2. Professor D. Swaminadhan, Proposal for Formation of the New Federal World Government.
   https://drive.google.com/file/d/15mrLdjos4vp5tbcdeuhtYEkStQzMWN_5/view?usp=sharing
3. Earth Constitution (www.earth-constitution.org).
4. The Constitution of India.

ABOUT THE BOOK

Two issues are bothering the humanity at present. First, the contemporary national and international scenarios in socioeconomic, political, ethnic, and cultural domains are throwing up many issues, problems, and challenges relating to development, environment, human rights, human security, communal harmony, peaceful coexistence amongst nations, and world peace and security. Second, existing global institutions are proving to be wanting in their structures and authorities in solving these problems. Alternatively, a new global independent organisation with enforcing authority is needed to act upon and solve these issues. The need for replacement of UNO seems to be justified because of failure to solve global problems. The nineteenth and twentieth centuries witnessed revivals of proposals for world government that were fuelled by positive developments— such as technological progress in travel and communications that enabled rapid economic globalization, as well as negative developments such as the devastating impact of wars fought with modern technology. The author's approach of the formation of the World Parliament is through proportional representation of nations' parliaments and thus avoids direct election process for its formation. All the nations and their people's representatives are involved in the formation of the World Parliament and the world government. Based on this line of thinking, the structure for a New Federal World Government and the New Federal World Constitution are presented in this book.

ABOUT THE AUTHOR

Professor D. SWAMINADHAN
PhD (England), D.Sc. (h/c), PhD (h/c), FIE, FNAE, FAPAS, FTAS, MISTE, MISCA, MIIPA
Global Chairman, World Intellectual Forum (WIF), Hyderabad, India
Chairman, Global Network for Peace, Disarmament and Development (GNET-PEDAD), Hyderabad, India
Former Member, National Advisory Council, Government of India, New Delhi
Former Member, Planning Commission, Govt. of India, New Delhi
Former Vice Chancellor, Jawaharlal Nehru Technological University (JNTU), Hyderabad, India
Former Vice Chairman, AP State Planning Board, Govt. of Andhra Pradesh, Hyderabad, India

Professor D. Swaminadhan, born on 01/02/1938, hails from Guntur, Andhra Pradesh, India. He is a distinguished educationist, engineer-scientist, researcher, and a planner. He obtained his PhD from the University of Liverpool (England). He worked as additional secretary in the University Grants Commission, New Delhi; as vice chancellor, Jawaharlal Nehru Technological University, Hyderabad; and as a member, Planning Commission, Government of India. He was also a UNESCO chair professor. Professor D. Swaminadhan has nearly fifty-five years of experience in the field of higher education, engineering, technical and management education, research, educational planning, and administration. He has a clear foresight about the dynamics of development of higher and technical education in the country. He is now global chair for World Intellectual Forum (WIF), Hyderabad, India. He is also chairman, Global Network for Peace, Disarmament, and Development (GNET-PEDAD), Hyderabad, India.

*****

INDEX

CPSIA information can be obtained
at www.ICGtesting.com
Printed in the USA
BVHW031000290319
544056BV00001B/117/P